CARLO ACUTIS

COURTNEY MARES

Carlo Acutis

A Saint in Sneakers

IGNATIUS PRESS SAN FRANCISCO

Except where noted, the Scripture citations used in this work are taken from the *Revised Standard Version of the Bible—Second Catholic Edition* (Ignatius Edition), copyright © 1965, 1966, 2006 National Council of the Churches of Christ in the United States of America. Used by permission. All rights reserved.

Excerpts from the English translation of the *Catechism of the Catholic Church* for use in the United States of America copyright © 1994, United States Catholic Conference, Inc.—Libreria Editrice Vaticana. English translation of the *Catechism of the Catholic Church: Modifications from the Editio Typica* copyright © 1997, United States Conference of Catholic Bishops—Libreria Editrice Vaticana.

Quotations from English translations of papal documents are from the Vatican website. © Libreria Editrice Vaticana. All rights reserved. Used with permission.

Except where noted, quotations from Italian sources have been translated into English by the author.

Cover photograph of Carlo Acutis was
used with the kind permission of the
Associazione Carlo Acutis, Assisi, Italy.

Cover design by Enrique J. Aguilar

ISBN 978-1-62164-813-0 (PB)
ISBN 978-1-64229-366-1 (eBook)
Library of Congress Control Number 2025932207
Printed in the United States of America ♾

For my godson, Rafael

Contents

The disciples came to Jesus, saying, "Who is the greatest in the kingdom of heaven?" And calling to him a child, he put him in the midst of them, and said, "Truly, I say to you, unless you turn and become like children, you will never enter the kingdom of heaven. Whoever humbles himself like this child, he is the greatest in the kingdom of heaven."

—Matthew 18:1–4

Introduction to the Updated Edition

Since this book was first published, Carlo Acutis' story has captivated and inspired people around the world. After his beatification in 2020, Carlo was hailed as a patron for the digital age and a model of holiness for the twenty-first century.

This updated edition of this book is being published at the momentous occasion of his canonization during the Catholic Church's 2025 Jubilee of Hope.

As the first millennial Catholic saint, Carlo's demonstrates by his life that sanctity is attainable in the modern world and that the Eucharist is, as he loved to say, the "highway to heaven".

The First Computer-Coding Saint

Carlo Acutis was an ordinary teenager with an extraordinary love for the Eucharist. He was a child of his time, fascinated by technology and drawn to the internet and computer coding. Though his life was brief—he died of leukemia in 2006 at the age of fifteen—Carlo's example left a profound influence on people of all ages. His unshakable devotion to the Real Presence of Jesus in the Eucharist, coupled with his kindness, humility, and joy, continues to inspire.

Hundreds of thousands of pilgrims have flocked to his tomb in Assisi, Italy, where he has been famously laid to rest in Nike sneakers—a visible reminder that holiness is possible for everyday people living in today's world. Catholic schools now bear his name in England, Mexico, Malawi,

Chile, Australia, and the United States. Statues and stained glass windows of Carlo adorn churches from Europe to the Americas. And his Eucharistic miracles exhibition has been displayed in thousands of parishes across the globe, including in the Philippines, Argentina, Vietnam, China, and Indonesia, spreading his message to millions.

Carlo's life exemplifies how faith can flourish in the digital era. As a patron of many ministries, his example has launched a wave of creative evangelization. New youth groups, online learning platforms, and digital initiatives now bear his name, carrying forward his mission to help more people to encounter Christ. Summer camps, such as Camp Carlo in the mountains of West Virginia, have been established to help young people grow in their faith, while comic books, documentaries, and even video games are being developed to tell his story in ways that resonate with new generations.

At the National Eucharistic Congress in Indianapolis in 2024, tens of thousands of people had the opportunity to venerate Carlo's relics. As a patron of this Eucharistic revival, Carlo's life serves as a reminder of the power of Eucharistic adoration and daily Mass to transform lives.

Beyond the initiatives and projects inspired by Carlo, his intercession has also touched individual lives in miraculous ways. Cancer survivors continue to call on Carlo for help, including Ellen Loesel, whose story opens chapter 1 of this book. Ellen has since given birth to a son, naming him Joseph Carlo in honor of the saint who interceded for her.

The Second Miracle

In 2024, Pope Francis recognized the second medical miracle attributed to Carlo's intercession, which was required for his canonization. The miracle involved the healing of a twenty-one-year-old Costa Rican student, Valeria Valverde, who suffered a severe head injury in a bicycle accident in Florence in 2022. After undergoing emergency surgery to relieve intracranial pressure, Valeria's condition was critical. Doctors warned her family that she could die at any moment.

In desperation and faith, six days after the accident, Valeria's mother left her daughter's bedside to embark on a pilgrimage to Assisi. She left a handwritten prayer at Carlo's tomb, asking for her daughter's healing. On that same day, Valeria began to breathe on her own, defying her doctors' expectations. By the next day, she regained movement in her arms and some speech. Within ten days, she was discharged from intensive care. Later medical tests revealed that the bleeding bruise in her brain had vanished entirely.

Valeria's recovery was so remarkable that it astonished her doctors. Contrary to medical predictions, she required only one week of physical therapy before resuming normal activities. Two months after her accident, she traveled with her mother on pilgrimage to Assisi to thank Carlo for his intercession, celebrating her complete healing—a healing inexplicable except as a miracle.

The Vatican's recognition of the miracle made possible Carlo's canonization as the first computer-coding saint in the history of the Catholic Church, which—as of the writing of this introduction—is scheduled to take place at the Vatican on Divine Mercy Sunday during a global gathering of teenagers for the 2025 Jubilee of Hope.

As you will see in this book, Carlo Acutis' story is one of faith and heroic virtue, proof of the transformative power of the Eucharist. He may be the first millennial saint, but he is surely not the last. Carlo's life and intercession remind us that sanctity is not reserved for centuries past or for those living in monasteries; it is possible here and now, even in a world saturated with distractions.

Carlo's example challenges all of us to embrace the Eucharist, which he called our "highway to heaven", and to use our unique talents for the greater glory of God. As his influence continues to grow, it is clear that Carlo Acutis is not only a saint for young people but for all who seek to find God in the everyday and to bring his light to others.

This updated biography invites readers to delve deeper into the life of this remarkable young Christian and to be inspired by his enduring message: that true happiness is found in Jesus, truly present in the Eucharist, and in sharing his love with the world.

I

Global "Influencer for God"

As Ellen Loesel walked through the threshold of an old church in an Italian hill town, she noticed a group of people gathered in the back corner of the sanctuary. A young man cried, a mother prayed while holding her children, and a Franciscan friar ushered high school students through the pews. All eyes were focused on a white stone tomb. Visible through a pane of glass on the tomb lay the body of a fifteen-year-old boy wearing jeans, a track jacket, and Nike sneakers. Etched in the stone below: *Carlo Acutis, 1991–2006.*

Ellen, too, was filled with emotion as she approached the tomb with her husband, Peter. She had first heard Carlo's story about a year earlier. At the time, she stuffed a holy card with a photo of Carlo in her prayer journal and then did not think much more about him—until she received her diagnosis.

Learning that you have breast cancer at twenty-five years old can feel like "a death sentence", Ellen said.[1] She found out that she had cancer while she was planning her wedding, three months after getting engaged. Her spiritual director and other Catholics in her community asked: "Who is your patron saint? Who are you asking intercession from?" Ellen considered a lot of Catholic saints whom she could call on while facing this terrible challenge, but Carlo Acutis "kept popping up".

Ellen remembers, for example, that "the prayer card that

I had just stuffed in my journal became the page that I was on in my journal." After researching more about Carlo's life, she saw new dimensions that she had not realized before, such as the boy's bravery while suffering from cancer and how he inspired his parents and relatives to return to church and discover a deeper faith in God. As she faced the possibility of her own death, she was struck by Carlo's "detachment from this life and his love for the next".

Throughout Ellen's battle with cancer and a wedding that took place days before she started chemotherapy, Carlo felt like a constant companion in her prayers. She decorated her new home with his quotes and photos to help give her strength. "His humility in his treatments was always something that I was trying to strive after, even though I was not humble or as peaceful as he was. . . . With cancer patients, there are a lot of reasons to be depressed, sad, and hopeless, but Carlo was calm and joyful."

To a non-Christian, it might seem strange that a cancer patient would find hope in the story of a boy who died all too young from cancer. When a child dies before his life has barely begun, it appears to many people to be a tragedy. Yet God uses all things for good.[2] This is the great paradox of Christianity. Through his death on the Cross, Jesus transformed suffering, offered for love, into a powerful force—"the power of salvific suffering".* Christ's death on the Cross is the ultimate paradox. His death destroyed death and brought life to the world. The instrument of death—the Cross—is now the way to life. A tree once brought death to Adam and Eve; now a tree brings life. What appeared to be the end was actually the beginning.

And God continues to work in mysterious ways. In the last days of his life, fifteen-year-old Carlo offered up for

* John Paul II, apostolic letter *Salvifici doloris* (February 11, 1984), no. 1.

others all the suffering he endured. And through his intercession, the Lord has worked miracles and touched countless lives around the world.

Ellen's story is just one from the crowds who approach Carlo's tomb each day, trusting God with their hopes and fears. Many more people have been moved by Carlo's story via the Internet.

Sainthood Gone Viral

When Carlo became the first millennial beatified by the Catholic Church, more people searched on Google for information about him than about the pope.[3] Along with Carlo's name, the term "eucharistic miracles" showed a massive increase in search frequency.[4] Amid the noise and the clutter of online pop-culture trends and political rants, people in Singapore, Canada, Ireland, India, and Argentina were searching for information about miracles, physical signs of God's presence on Earth. How is it that a boy from Milan who lived only to the age of fifteen came to be a global "influencer for God"[5] more than a decade after he died?

Born in 1991, the same year as the launch of the World Wide Web, Carlo came into the world amid a digital information revolution. The innovations created by Tim Berners-Lee and a team of researchers in Geneva, Switzerland—URLs, HTML, HTTP—were to become the building blocks of what would connect the world.[6] The invention of the Web changed the way that Carlo's generation and the generations that followed accessed information, communicated with each other, and learned about the world around them.

As a computer-programming millennial on the path to sainthood, Carlo has shown that Apple computers, Spider-man comics, and Super Mario on Nintendo 64 and a life of heroic virtue are not mutually exclusive. On the surface, much of Carlo's life appears quite ordinary. He was a tech-savvy kid who went to school, attended Mass, and enjoyed playing video games. He did not seek attention for himself, yet his witness and enthusiastic conversations about God inspired adults to convert and be baptized. While he was still an elementary school student, he sold his toys to give to the poor and gave up eating the chocolate hazelnut spread Nutella as a sacrifice offered up for others.[7] In high school, he courageously defended controversial Church teachings in conversations with friends and in the classroom, leading many of his classmates to testify that he helped them to grow in faith.

Those who knew Carlo before he departed the world in 2006 will tell you that his true passion was the Real Presence of Jesus in the Eucharist. His daily prayer before the tabernacle was the foundation for everything in his life. Carlo called the Eucharist "my highway to heaven",[8] and he did all in his power to make Christ's Real Presence known. His spiritual director has recalled that Carlo was convinced that the evidence of Eucharistic miracles could be persuasive in helping people to realize that Jesus is present at every Mass.[9] This simple idea inspired an international exhibition on eucharistic miracles that has reached thousands of people across the globe, fulfilling Carlo's dream of making Christ's presence known.

2

A Great Grace

Jesus said to his disciples, "I thank you, Father, Lord of heaven and earth, that you have hidden these things from the wise and understanding and revealed them to infants" (Mt 11:25). The birth of every child is a gift, but for Antonia Salzano, the arrival of her firstborn was a great grace. Her little son, full of innocent curiosity about life's biggest questions, would lead her—and later, many others—back to God.

Carlo's mother, like many of her generation in Italy, grew up immersed in a culture full of the vestiges of a long Catholic tradition. Antonia's family lived in the center of Rome, near Piazza Venezia, not far from grand basilicas that hold the tombs of Jesus' apostles and the relics of early Roman martyrs.[1] Yet faith did not directly affect her daily decision-making. Mass attendance was for weddings and funerals, but it was by no means a weekly practice. In her testimony to the Vatican, Antonia wrote that her family was not "hostile" to the faith but "had little affinity for religious practice".[2] She went years without attending Sunday Mass.

Antonia met Andrea Acutis in a seaside town in northern Tuscany in the summer of 1986. Andrea was the son of a wealthy family from Turin, Italy, and was a student of economics at the University of Geneva in Switzerland.[3] Within one year, the two were engaged.[4]

Andrea grew up in a more religious family than Antonia's and attended Mass as a child, but he stopped practicing the faith when he was in college.[5] He began military service after graduating from college, first in the Alpine Corps in Aosta, a mountainous region in northwest Italy, and later with the Carabinieri Corps in Rome. After his military service, Andrea landed a job as an investment banker in London with the corporate finance firm Lazard Brothers.[6] He relocated to England, and Antonia followed him.

The two married in Rome in the Basilica of Saint Apollinaris, near Piazza Navona, on January 27, 1990.[7] Antonia was twenty-three, and Andrea was twenty-five. The newlyweds settled in an apartment in London's upscale Knightsbridge neighborhood, near Hyde Park and Harrod's department store.

A Baby with Big Brown Eyes

A little more than one year after they were married, Andrea and Antonia welcomed their first child—a son with big brown eyes, born in London's Portland Hospital at 11:00 A.M. on May 3, 1991. He weighed a little under eight pounds and was about twenty-two inches long.[8] The happy parents named him Carlo, after the baby's paternal grandfather, Carlo Acutis Sr., who was also selected to be his godfather.

Carlo's grandfather had built a successful career in the insurance business during Italy's "economic miracle" in the decades following World War II. He rose to senior management for the Toro Insurance company and in 1986 bought the controlling stake of Vittoria Insurance, where he served as president.[9] Carlo Acutis Sr. had married Maria Henrietta

Perłowska, whose grandfather had worked as a diplomat in Poland's embassy to the Holy See.* Carlo's parents selected his maternal grandmother, Luana, to be his godmother.[10] She would later come to live with the Acutis family after her husband died in 1995. She helped raise Carlo from the age of four onward.[11]

"Carlo, I Baptize You . . ."

The grandparents on both sides of the family traveled to London and were present at their grandson's Baptism in the Church of Our Lady of Dolours on Fulham Road in Chelsea. Father Nicholas Martin, O.S.M., baptized Carlo on May 18, 1991, fifteen days after he was born. Little Carlo was dressed in a white gown, a symbol of Jesus' Resurrection.

Under the gaze of a statue of Our Lady of Fátima, Father Martin made the sign of the cross, symbolizing the grace of redemption Christ won through his Passion and death. Pouring water over Carlo's head, the priest said: "Carlo, I baptize you in the name of the Father, and of the Son, and of the Holy Spirit." Baby Carlo was anointed with sacred chrism, a consecrated perfumed oil and thus entered

* Carlo's paternal grandmother was part Irish and part Polish, making Carlo a little bit Polish and Irish. Maria Henrietta Perłowska was the granddaughter of Ambassador Jan Perłowski, who had served as counsel to the Polish Mission to the Holy See during the pontificate of Pius XI before becoming a knight of the pontifical orders of Saint Gregory the Great and of Saint Sylvester. Carlo's mother has also pointed out that there are saints on her branch of the family tree: Saint Catherine Volpicelli (1839–1894) on her mother's side and Saint Giulia Salzano (1846–1929) on her father's side. Salzano Acutis and Rodari, *Il segreto*, 86.

through the Holy Spirit into Christ's threefold mission of priest, prophet, and king.[12]

Like all men, Carlo was born with a fallen human nature, separated from God because of Original Sin. Through his Baptism, Carlo was born anew into the Mystical Body of Christ. By baptizing Carlo, the Acutis family gave their son a great gift. Their infant son was reborn as a son of God, freed from sin and able to enter the kingdom of heaven. This sacrament opened the door to all the other life-giving sacraments in the Catholic Church, and Carlo would come to see his reception of them as the most important moments of his life.

Carlo would later tell his parents: "I will never stop thanking Jesus for having given us such a great gift by giving us the sacrament of Baptism."* The Acutis family celebrated the Baptism with a white cake baked in the shape of a lamb.[13]

The Move to Milan

A few months after Carlo's Baptism, the Acutis family moved back to Italy so that Andrea could work in Milan as an executive at Vittoria Insurance, the company owned by Carlo's grandfather.[14] Milan had firmly established itself as the financial hub of Italy from the previous decade of economic growth. If Rome was the Italian capital of all things ancient, Catholic, and beautiful, Milan was the Italian capital of business, luxury, and style. It is said that for every Catholic church in Rome, there is a bank in Milan. The

* According to his parents, Carlo was nine years old when he said this after a Mass at his parish in which the parishioners renewed their baptismal promises. Carbone, *Originali o fotocopie*, 45, quoting *Positio*, 291.

stylish northern Italian city had gained renown as the headquarters of the fashion empires of Giorgio Armani, Dolce & Gabbana, Prada, and Versace.

Amid this economic bustle, the city's centuries-old churches and buildings that survived the bombing and destruction of World War II still served as a reminder that Catholic giants such as Saint Ambrose and Saint Charles Borromeo, both bishops of Milan, had once walked its streets.*

The Acutis family settled in Milan's Porta Magenta district, not far from Santa Maria delle Grazie, the church in which Leonardo da Vinci's expansive mural of the Last Supper is found. The neighborhood was filled with elegant old buildings and wide, tree-lined streets. It was residential yet centrally located. Some of the historic buildings were ivy covered; others had iron gates leading to lush interior courtyards filled with hydrangeas. A yellow trolley passed along tracks in front of the Acutis family home.

Carlo and the Nanny with the Holy Cards

When Carlo was three years old, his family hired a young Polish girl named Beata to serve as a nanny for him.[15] Antonia vividly remembers that Beata arrived at the family's Milan apartment for her first day of work with "a bag full of holy cards".[16]

Beata was what Carlo's mother described as a "devotee" of Pope John Paul II.[17] The pope from the small town of Wadowice, Poland, had gained the world's attention with his

* Milan is also the city where Saint Augustine experienced his conversion and was baptized in 387.

bold leadership in the face of the communist threat during the Cold War. He had been a beacon of hope to those under the atheist rule of the Soviets, and he attracted hundreds of thousands of people to an outdoor Mass in Warsaw, then a Soviet-controlled city.[18] By the early 1990s, Pope John Paul II had been the head of the Catholic Church for more than a decade, and the once seemingly unstoppable USSR had dissolved.

Carlo's Polish nanny was likely the first person to take him with her to Mass regularly and to teach him the basics of the Catholic faith. When Carlo was a toddler, Beata taught him to stop inside churches to "greet Jesus". Among the holy cards that Beata had brought, little Carlo cherished the ones depicting the Blessed Virgin Mary at shrines in Poland.[19]

The Acutis family had hired several nannies to care for Carlo before finding Beata, but none of them had as close a connection with their son. "It was 'love at first sight' between Carlo and me", Beata said in her testimony to the Vatican Dicastery for the Causes of Saints. "The relationship was strong until his death."[20]

Devotion to the Rosary

Carlo was enrolled in the Parco Pagani preschool in Milan in 1995 when he was four years old. Beata would take him to school with his rosary in hand. She recalled, "We said the Rosary together . . . when I accompanied him [to school]. He was proud to be able to show his schoolmates his rosary as a sign of his firm faith, yet he was just a child."[21] Praying the Rosary immersed Carlo from a young age in the mysteries of Jesus' life and the history of salvation. Saint John Paul II wrote that reciting the Rosary puts one "in living communion with Jesus through . . . the heart of his Mother".[22]

Beata, who stayed with the Acutis family until Carlo turned six, helped establish the Rosary as part of his daily routine. She remembered that "the Rosary was the daily prayer, every evening, and it often happened that in the morning, when making his bed, he would find his rosary between the sheets because he had fallen asleep while he was saying it."[23]

In the years that Beata was employed by the Acutis family,* she prayed the Rosary with little Carlo and took him to visit Marian shrines, including the Shrine of Our Lady of Pompeii, which contains a revered painting of Our Lady of the Rosary.† It was at this shrine that Carlo would later make his first consecration to Mary, in 1996 at the age of five, entrusting himself to Our Lady of the Rosary.[24]

"One of his favorite gifts for anyone who came to his house was a rosary", Beata recalled.[25]

A "Little Savior"

Carlo's mother noticed a budding piety in her son when he was in preschool. "I remember when he was very young and

* According to the Vatican's *Positio*, Beata worked for the Acutis family from 1994 to 1997. See Congregatio de Causis Sanctorum, *Mediolanensis beatificationis et canonizationis servi Dei Carlo Acutis, Christifidelis laici (1991–2006): Positio super vita, virtutibus et fama sanctitatis* (Romae, 2017), 151.

† Saint John Paul II had an image of Our Lady of Pompeii brought to the Vatican when he signed his apostolic letter on the Rosary, which introduced the Luminous Mysteries of the Rosary.

we were passing in front of churches, he wanted to go in and greet the crucified Jesus in the tabernacle."[26] The little boy would collect spring flowers to bring to Our Lady, as Beata taught him,[27] placing them before a statue of the Virgin Mary. His mother also recalls his affectionately kissing a statue of baby Jesus at Christmastime.[28] Carlo asked his parents to pray a nighttime prayer with him before bed.* His parents bought him a little white stuffed lamb that young Carlo became attached to, keeping it as he grew older "because it reminded him of Jesus".[29]

Antonia remembers showing Carlo, when he was four years old, a medal that his great-grandmother had given him at his Baptism. It depicted the Sacred Heart of Jesus on one side and the Immaculate Heart of Mary on the other. Carlo asked to wear the medal and told his mother: "This way, Jesus and Our Lady will always be close to my heart!"[30]

Children are natural philosophers, often asking their parents big questions. Carlo's mother has said that her son was always asking her questions about the Catholic faith. She said: "I grew up in a secular family, as millions of people do, I suppose. So having this son who insistently asked me questions about the faith forced me to reflect."[31] Antonia said that faced with these questions as a non-practicing Catholic, she felt "illiterate" about the Catholic faith.[32] She sought out a priest who could help answer Carlo's questions, which had also become her own questions.

Antonia's friend recommended to her a priest who lived in Bologna, Father Ilio Carrai. Antonia made the first trip to visit him in the spring of 1995, when Carlo had just

* Carlo was about four years old at this time, according to Carbone, *Originali o Fotocopie*, 143.

turned four.[33] After learning more about the why behind Catholicism, Antonia was slowly drawn to the Church and the sacraments.* Reflecting on this life-changing series of events, she said, "I always say that Carlo was a little savior for me."[34]

* Antonia has said that Beata also helped her to grow in her faith, particularly when Antonia's father died suddenly of a heart attack. Salzano Acutis and Rodari, *Il segreto*, 111.

3

A Nineties Kid

Though Carlo had expressed a special affinity for Catholicism at a very young age, he was not a lofty personage above his nose-picking kindergarten peers. He was a nineties kid who loved watching VHS tapes, dressing up as Spiderman, trading Pokémon cards, and playing on his computer and his PlayStation.

Children in the 1990s had no iPhones or tablets and knew nothing of YouTube, Facebook, or Netflix—these things did not yet exist. The millennial generation—people born between 1981 and 1996[1]—would eventually upgrade to cell phones and social media as teenagers and young adults, but it was not until 2003 that a majority of Americans—62 percent—owned a basic cell phone.[2] In the nineties, kids played with action figures, used their imaginations, watched cartoons, and ran around neighborhood playgrounds.

An Only Child

Like a fair number of millennials, Carlo grew up without any siblings. Both his parents worked for much of his childhood, and he was left in the care of the family's staff, who usually took him to and from school. His mother worked in her family's publishing company, and his father worked long hours as an insurance-company executive.[3] As an only child, Carlo learned how to make his own fun. His mother remembers that he could spend hours playing alone without getting into trouble. He was content to sit and play with his Legos or draw his favorite cartoon characters.

By all accounts, Carlo was a naturally sanguine kid. Those closest to him have said that he was friendly and affectionate, always ready with a kind greeting and a smile for a stranger. Vatican records describe Carlo as having a "serene and affable temperament and an open and jovial character" from early childhood.[4] His mother recalls, "My son was always sociable, lively, playful, open to everyone. . . . With us, he was very obedient. I can truly say that I never had any problems with him. He was always willing to do anything we asked of him."[5]

Carlo's parents enrolled him in many sports, but he did not take any of them particularly seriously. Throughout his school years, he tried karate, tennis, volleyball, swimming, and soccer.[6] His mother said that Carlo was "quite bad at soccer, but he loved being with friends".[7] Carlo's paternal grandparents, who had a house in Switzerland near the Gstaad ski resort, were particularly adamant that Carlo learn how to ski. When the family visited during winter vacation, they enrolled Carlo in two weeks of ski lessons, after which he competed in a small ski race, placing second.[8]

The Acutis family hired a young man named Rajesh Mohur in December 1995 to help take care of Carlo. Rajesh had come to Italy from the island of Mauritius, and his first impression of Carlo, with his brown curly hair, was that he looked like the little cherubs seen in paintings and sculptures around Milan. On his second day working for the family, Rajesh remembers that little Carlo approached him with a big smile and a gift—a piece of chewing gum.[9]

On rainy days, Carlo would sometimes watch videotapes

of cartoons based on the Bible and the lives of the saints together with Rajesh, who watched with some interest because he had not had much exposure to Catholicism. Rajesh remembers that some of Carlo's other favorite cartoons as a kid were the Transformers, Batman, Spiderman, Pokémon, and the Smurfs (called "I Puffi" in Italian).

Carlo's favorite book as a child was *The Little Prince* by French author Antoine de Saint-Exupéry. In the book, a mysterious little prince, full of depth, comes to Earth from a faraway planet. After arriving on Earth, the prince learns that the secret to life is very simple: "One sees clearly only with the heart. Anything essential is invisible to the eyes."* Early in life, Carlo, too, would learn to put into practice this principle by choosing to spend his free time in prayer, aware of God's invisible presence, knowing that, with God, he was never alone.

Elementary School with the Marcelline Sisters

Carlo was fortunate to be able to walk to school in less than five minutes. The Tommaseo Institute, where he studied for eight years of both elementary and middle school, was around the corner from the Acutis family's apartment. Rajesh, who accompanied Carlo on these daily walks, has said that little Carlo often asked to stop and pray in the Catholic church that they passed on the way. The church, Santa Maria Segreta, was Carlo's parish. It was conveniently located across the street from his school and separated by a courtyard with park benches and cherry trees that bloomed

* This quote is engraved on one of the panels in the display above Carlo Acutis' tomb in Assisi. (See chapter 15 for more details.) Antoine de Saint-Exupéry, *The Little Prince* (San Diego: Harvest, 2000), 63.

every spring. His parish and his Catholic school were two of the most formative places in Carlo's life.

The Marcelline Sisters, a religious order dedicated to education, ran the Tommaseo Institute. Blessed Father Luigi Biraghi, who established several Catholic schools in and around Milan, founded the Marcelline congregation in 1838.* The elementary school had been around for nearly one hundred years by the time Carlo enrolled.[10] Its entrance hall was painted blue and adorned with golden *M*s in honor of the Virgin Mary.

Carlo was known among his elementary school teachers for his kindness and his eagerness to help his classmates. "A true budding gentleman", one teacher commented.[11] Sister Isa Velate, who taught religion at the school, remembers that Carlo was a "very generous" child who did not hesitate to share with his classmates. Sister Maria del Rocío Soria Ratia recalls that Carlo loved to make jokes.[12]

Carlo's parents had originally enrolled him in the San Carlo Institute in Milan, a private school for kindergarten through high school located in the sixteenth-century Busca Arconati Visconti Palace across from the basilica that contains Leonardo da Vinci's *Last Supper*. After Carlo had attended for only two months, however, the family decided to transfer him to the Tommaseo Institute, which was closer to the family's apartment.[13] Thanks to his cheerful temperament and his amiable and positive attitude, Carlo had no trouble adapting to his new elementary school and quickly made new friends.[14]

Valentina, one of Carlo's elementary school teachers at Tommaseo, said that she always "put her worst-behaved

* Father Biraghi was beatified in Milan on April 30, 2006, when Carlo was in high school.

students" next to Carlo during school prayers or Masses with the hope that his good example would rub off on them.[15] But the teacher also noted that some of Carlo's classmates sought to take advantage of his generosity. She scolded students who repeatedly asked seven-year-old Carlo for money to buy a snack when she saw that Carlo would give them all he had. Seeing that his classmates were getting punished, Carlo told his teacher not to worry: "I wasn't hungry today anyway."[16]

Summer Vacation by the Sea

Like many kids in Italy, Carlo's childhood was filled with summers playing at the beach. During summer vacation, his parents would send him to stay with his maternal grandparents on the Cilento coast, about seventy-five miles south of the Amalfi coast.[17]

In the small village of Centola, Carlo could play among the rocks and in the sea. He loved the sea and sea life, particularly dolphins. He had first encountered dolphins on a special birthday trip with his parents to an amusement park called Gardaland near Lake Garda in Northern Italy.[18] After this encounter, little Carlo decided that dolphins were among his favorite animals, although he had a love and sensitivity for all animals.

While staying with his maternal grandparents in a small town in Southern Italy, Carlo was immersed in a culture that was different in many ways from that of the fast-paced city center where he grew up and went to school. Italian culture places importance on taking vacations and spending time with family. Many Italians take several weeks off from work in August, at a time called *Ferragosto*, a public holiday celebrated throughout Italy. And in beach towns in the south of Italy near his grandparents' house, the feast of the Assumption of Mary on August 15 was celebrated with great pomp, with dramatic fireworks displays and religious processions.

The 1990s were already an era of distraction in many ways. Technology made it possible for kids to be entertained by television cartoons, computer programs, and video games for hours, yet young Carlo did not let screens distract him from pursuing a deep desire of his heart. In 1998, as he approached the age of seven, which the Catholic Church has traditionally identified as "the age of reason", he had already expressed a desire to deepen his relationship with the Lord. He asked his parents if he could receive his First Communion.

4

Highway to Heaven

The world's first highway was built in Italy in 1924. Engineer Piero Puricelli foresaw the need for a paved road reserved exclusively for motor traffic at a time when only one out of every thousand people in Italy owned a car. The Autostrada dei Laghi stretched from Milan to Varese and took fifteen months to build. It was a gateway from the urban northern capital to the scenic lakes region, later connecting the city to the stunning vistas of Lake Como.

As the Acutis family drove along the roads that make up this historic highway network in June 1998, Carlo prepared himself to receive the Blessed Sacrament for the first time.[1] Carlo would come to call the Eucharist "my highway to heaven".[2] The boy understood the Eucharist to be a speedway to holiness, or, as Saint Pius X is reputed to have said: "Holy Communion is the shortest and safest way to Heaven."*

First Communion

Carlo's parents obtained special permission for their son to receive his First Communion in a private ceremony at a cloistered convent when he was seven years old. Carlo had expressed his strong desire to receive the Eucharist to his

* Saint Pius X also lowered the minimum age for children to receive First Communion to seven years old.

nanny, Beata, who said: "He was sorry not to be able to receive Communion when he saw that I was going to the altar. I know that Carlo wanted to receive Communion before the usual age because he desired it so much. He wanted to be like the Communion he received. Convinced that only if you are truly worthy and pure can you be in communion with Jesus, he wanted to be worthy and pure for Jesus."[3]

Father Aldo Locatelli, a priest who had helped Carlo's mother answer her son's many theological questions, requested that Archbishop Emeritus Pasquale Macchi* interview Carlo to assess whether he was prepared to receive the Blessed Sacrament.[4] The retired archbishop granted his approval, and the First Communion date was set for the Tuesday after the solemnity of Corpus Christi, the feast of the Body and Blood of Christ, instituted in the thirteenth century after a eucharistic miracle occurred in Bolsena, Italy.

The convent where Carlo received his First Communion was home to a five-hundred-year-old contemplative order of Ambrosian nuns, the Romite Sisters of Saint Ambrose ad Nemus (Saint Ambrose in the Woods), founded by Blessed Caterina Moriggi after a vision of the crucified Jesus inspired her to start a community of female hermits in the mountains of Varese, Italy, in the fifteenth century.† On the drive north of Milan through the scenic hills surrounding Lake Como, near the convent in Perego, the Acutis family stopped their car to let a shepherd cross the road with a

* The late Archbishop Macchi was the archbishop of Loreto and was the former private secretary of Pope Paul VI. He had been a resident at the Romite Sisters' convent since his retirement in 1996.

† Blessed Caterina Moriggi (1437–1478) dedicated her life to the service of God at the age of fourteen. After losing her entire family in a plague when she was a child, the orphaned girl consecrated her virginity to God and shortly thereafter received a vision of the crucified Jesus, which inspired her to start a community of female hermits in the mountains of Varese, Italy.

lamb. Carlo's mother has said that the young boy saw this as "a sign of predilection from the Lord" before his First Communion.[5]

Mother Maria Emanuele, the religious superior of the contemplative Ambrosian community told Carlo's postulator for beatification, Nicola Gori, about her memory of the First Communion at the convent:

> Composed and calm during the time of Holy Mass, he began to show signs of impatience as the moment of receiving Holy Communion approached. With Jesus in his heart, after holding his head in his hands for a short time in a recollected attitude, he began to move as if he could no longer keep still. It seemed that something had happened within him, known only to him, something too great for him to contain.[6]

The Ambrosian sisters kept Carlo in their prayers throughout his life, particularly as he prepared for the Sacrament of Confirmation, and the Acutis family returned to visit the convent several times over the years.[7] Carlo would go on to call the cloistered sisters "my guardian angels on Earth".[8]

Carlo's Parish: "Holy Mary of the Secret"

A few days after his First Communion, Carlo told his mother: "To always be united to Jesus: this is my life plan."[9] To accomplish this, Carlo wanted to attend daily Mass as often as possible. In Italy, many churches offer daily Masses in the evening at six or seven o'clock. The proximity of Carlo's parish allowed him to pause his homework or games to walk to Mass, accompanied by Rajesh.

Carlo's mother recalls that he often attended these evening Masses at their parish, Santa Maria Segreta. The church's name means "Holy Mary of the Secret".* The grand white church had a neobaroque facade with a marble statue of the Madonna and Child above its main entrance.† According to the parish, the "secret" refers to Jesus hidden in the young Blessed Virgin Mary's womb. For Carlo, this secret was also hidden in the church's tabernacle, where humble consecrated eucharistic hosts held Christ's Body, Blood, Soul, and Divinity.

"For my son, the presence of Jesus in the tabernacle was comparable to a very powerful magnet", Antonia said.[10] Carlo spent most of his prayer time in church, in the presence of Christ, rather than at home, according to Rajesh. Kneeling in one of the front rows of Santa Maria Segreta, Carlo prayed before a green marble altar, above which hung a red lamp to alert visitors to Christ's presence in the tabernacle. Inside the church, the city sounds of passing cars, motorbikes, and trolley cars could only faintly be heard. In this secret, sacred place, Carlo's life was "hidden with Christ" as he prayed.

When Monsignor Gianfranco Poma entered Santa Maria Segreta Church for the first time on a July afternoon in 2000, he noticed a nine-year-old boy kneeling in prayer in front of the tabernacle of the empty church. "It was my first day as parish priest", Poma recalled.[11] "So I approached him and

* The church's name came from another ancient Catholic church built in Milan on the location of a former Roman temple dedicated to Ceres.

† Santa Maria Segreta was built and rebuilt multiple times over the centuries before it was demolished and rebuilt again in the early twentieth century. Blessed Cardinal Andrea Carlo Ferrari, the archbishop of Milan, laid the first stone of the church in 1911. When its construction was completed in 1935, the parish church had a bell tower on either side, columns, cherubs, and niches containing statues of saints in a neobaroque style. The church's curved ceiling was decorated with early twentieth-century paintings of the life of the Virgin Mary.

asked, 'Do you sometimes come here to pray in front of the Eucharist?'" Carlo replied, "Yes, every now and then I come to tell my things to Jesus."[12]

Carlo believed that prayer during daily Mass was the best time to ask for God's help. He told his parents: "The decisive moment to ask the Lord for graces is at the Consecration, during the eucharistic celebration, when the Lord Jesus Christ offers himself to the Father."[13] He also held that it was very important always to make an act of thanksgiving after receiving Communion.[14] One parishioner who often attended the evening Mass at Santa Maria Segreta said: "I remember with so much sweetness this beautiful boy who approached the altar to receive Jesus with so much love."[15]

The Ambrosian Rite

Some may be surprised to learn that Carlo did not usually attend Mass in the Roman Rite, the rite offered in most Catholic churches around the world. Growing up in the Archdiocese of Milan, Carlo attended Mass in the Ambrosian Rite, one of the few ancient Western liturgical rites within the Latin Church.*

The Ambrosian Rite is the principal liturgical rite offered in the Archdiocese of Milan, which has more than 5.4 million inhabitants, as well as in some parishes in parts of Northern Italy and Lugano, Switzerland.[16] The Ambrosian Rite has been described as a "Christocentric" liturgy. Local tradition holds that the liturgy developed out of Saint

* The Catholic Church is home to twenty-four *sui iuris*, or self-governing, churches, all in communion with one another and under the primacy of the pope. Among the churches, there are different liturgical rites, including other Western rites within the Latin Church besides the Roman Rite.

Ambrose's response to the late fourth-century Arian heresy that denied Jesus' divinity.[17] The liturgy has a few key differences, meaning that Carlo's experience of the Mass was slightly different from that of Catholics who attend the Roman Rite. For example, the Kyrie Eleison is prayed at the end of Mass before the final blessing rather than at the beginning of Mass. The Ambrosian liturgy also does not contain the Agnus Dei (Lamb of God) prayer, and the sign of peace happens at the beginning of the Liturgy of the Eucharist, rather than right after the Eucharistic prayers. After the Second Vatican Council, some changes were made to the liturgy, which is now primarily offered in the Italian language.

The Ambrosian Rite uses a different lectionary, so Carlo would have heard a different cycle of readings at daily Mass. The liturgical calendar also differs, with six weeks of Advent and a Lent that does not include Ash Wednesday. In Ordinary Time, between Pentecost and October, priests wear red rather than green.

Certain days in the Ambrosian Rite require abstaining from the Eucharist. On Fridays in Lent, Mass is not offered, and the reception of the Eucharist is not allowed. This draws attention to the emptiness and loss caused by Christ's death on the Cross. A large wooden cross is placed on the altar to facilitate prayerful meditation on Christ's Passion.

The liturgy takes its name from Saint Ambrose, a towering figure in the Church in Milan.* The fourth-century bishop

* Saint Ambrose was one of the first Doctors of the Church, along with Saints Augustine, Gregory the Great, and Jerome. Ambrose served as the governor of the region in the year 374, when a crowd of Milanese Catholics called for him to become their bishop. Peter R. L. Brown, "St. Ambrose", *Encyclopedia Britannica*, last updated January 1, 2023, https://www.britannica.com/biography/Saint-Ambrose.

of Milan, who baptized Saint Augustine, lived simply and wrote prolifically, including composing several hymns. The tomb of the great saint and Doctor of the Church, in the Basilica of Saint Ambrose, was only a fifteen-minute walk from the Acutises' apartment. Saint Charles Borromeo,* another great bishop of Milan, defended the retention of the Ambrosian Rite during the Council of Trent in the sixteenth century. Borromeo is buried in Milan's cathedral, the Basilica of the Nativity of Saint Mary.

Seek First the Kingdom

Carlo's devotion to the Mass inevitably brought his family closer to the Church. Whenever the Acutis family was traveling, the first thing that Carlo would ask was where they might attend Mass near the hotel so that he would not miss an opportunity to receive Holy Communion.[18] "He was very keen on this encounter with Jesus, who, for him, was a living presence; he was a friend", his mother said.[19] When Carlo visited his grandparents at the seaside near Salerno, he made an impression on them by seeking to attend Mass before he went to the beach.[20] Carlo's enthusiasm for the faith was contagious. Luana, his grandmother and godmother, testified: "Neither I nor his parents were practicing before Carlo led us to the faith. He was the one who led us to God, to faith. . . .[21] I must admit that for most of my life . . . I was not a good Catholic, and thanks to Carlo, who, from a young age, asked me to go to Mass with him and his mother, I rediscovered the faith that had been lost in me", she said.[22]

* In Italy, he is known as Carlo Borromeo, or simply as San Carlo.

Shortly after receiving his First Communion, Carlo insisted that his entire family make a consecration to the Sacred Heart together.[23] Images of Jesus' Sacred Heart* abounded in Carlo's neighborhood in Milan, home to the Catholic University of the Sacred Heart. In the Basilica of Saint Ambrose, a larger-than-life marble statue of Jesus with his Sacred Heart ablaze extends his arm as an invitation to come to the tabernacle and pray for a while. The altar below is engraved with an image of Jesus and his disciples at the Last Supper. Carlo often liked to repeat: "The Sacred Heart of Jesus is the Eucharist."[24]

Carlo liked to attend Mass at the Dominican monastery of Santa Maria delle Grazie, where Leonardo da Vinci painted his *Last Supper*. Da Vinci's fresco, painted on the wall of the fifteenth-century monastery's refectory, is one of the most well-known pieces of art in the world, and it was just a few blocks away from the Acutis family's Milan apartment. The dramatic fresco depicts Christ's institution of the Eucharist, the inauguration of the liturgical event that was a focal point of Carlo's daily life.

Carlo's mother also accompanied him to daily Mass at a Carmelite church in Milan not far from the Acutis residence, and there Carlo befriended a Carmelite priest. The church was dedicated to Corpus Christi (the Body of Christ), one of Carlo's favorite holy days.[25] Thanks to his friendship with the local Carmelites, Carlo began to wear a scapular when he was about seven years old.[26] This sacramental, worn under

* Devotion to the Sacred Heart of Jesus was promoted by Saint Margaret Mary Alacoque, a seventeenth-century French nun who experienced visions of Christ's Sacred Heart for eighteen months. Pope Leo XIII consecrated the entire world to the Sacred Heart of Jesus in 1899. In his encyclical *Annum sacrum*, Pope Leo XIII described the act of consecration as one that could "draw tighter the bonds which naturally connect public affairs with God".

his shirt, signified his devotion to the Blessed Virgin Mary and his trust in her motherly protection.

Jesus Remains with Us in the Tabernacle

Carlo's catchphrase, "the Eucharist is my highway to heaven",[27] sums up the centrality of the Eucharist in Carlo's spiritual life. Father Ilio Carrai, his spiritual director,* attested that Carlo loved Saint Ignatius of Antioch's description of the Eucharist as the "medicine of immortality".[28] He said that Carlo believed that when people receive Communion daily, they "are quickly sanctified and strengthened and they risk less to fall into dangerous situations that can jeopardize their eternal salvation".[29] His grandmother noted that Carlo "always said that Communion is the most powerful medicine for the soul".[30] She added: "In fact, I have always thought that his charisma came from his daily Communion."

Carlo was convinced that "many people do not really understand the value of the Holy Mass." He said that if they did, they would realize "our great fortune in having God give Himself to us in the Consecrated Host . . . [and] would go to church every day to take part in the eucharistic celebration, renouncing many superfluous things."[31]

Carlo was confused by the priorities of some of his peers, who sometimes took their obsessions with sports or music to extremes. He told his mother, "People stand in long lines to see rock concerts or go to soccer games but would never think of standing in line before the Blessed Sacrament."[32] Andrea, Carlo's father, recalls that when he asked his son if

* See chapter 11 of this book for more on Father Carrai.

he wanted to participate in a pilgrimage to the Holy Land, Carlo's response caught him by surprise. His son replied:

> I prefer to stay in Milan because there are so many tabernacles in the churches where I can go and find Jesus at any time, and therefore I don't feel the need to go to Jerusalem. If Jesus remains with us always, wherever there is a consecrated Host, what need is there to make a pilgrimage to Jerusalem to visit the places where Jesus lived two thousand years ago? We should then visit the tabernacles with the same devotion.[33]

Carlo's parents remember that he once told them: "Jesus is Love, and the more we feed on him who becomes food and drink for us through the Eucharist, which truly contains his Body, Blood, Soul, and Divinity, the more our capacity to love increases."[34]

5

From Hinduism to Catholicism

Rajesh Mohur grew up on a small island in the Indian Ocean off the coast of Africa, about five hundred miles east of Madagascar. Like most of Mauritius' population, Rajesh was a Hindu. He grew up speaking Creole and studying Sanskrit, the ancient language used in Hindu scriptures.

The Mohur family was of the Brahman priestly caste, the highest of the four castes in Hindu society. Rajesh's father was a Hindu priest who served as the president of the Hindu Association in Mauritius. Rajesh recalls: "[My father] used to teach me from the early beginning about all of their prayers . . . about the scriptures, Indian scriptures."*

At the age of sixteen, Rajesh's father sent him to India to continue his education in Gujarat, the city where Mahatma Gandhi was born. During his time in India, Rajesh was even more fully immersed in Hindu culture and religious practice. "I've been to so many temples. I met so many gurus in the meditation center, and I met swamis", Rajesh said. "I witnessed all of those places. It was peaceful, you know. Nice. But your life doesn't change. . . . I was in search of a living God."

Rajesh was also unsettled by the deep divide between the rich and the poor he witnessed at Hindu temples in India.

* Rajesh Mohur, interview by author, Milan, Italy, August 3, 2021. All quotations from Rajesh Mohur in this chapter are from the August 2021 interview, unless otherwise noted.

> The rich, when they go to pray, you know, they can afford the milk, flowers. All of those things, they just get wasted on those idols. I don't blame them. But when they come out [of the temple] there are so many people, poor people, outside the [temple] that were waiting for something to eat or drink or to have some money to buy some food, but they were ignored. . . . What I had learned from my dad, what he taught me, and what I have experienced in India—these were completely different.

This left Rajesh feeling empty inside. He said, "My journey was always to find something that . . . from myself, deep down, I could not fulfill."

After he was accepted to a university in Rajasthan, Rajesh ended up staying in India, where he completed a bachelor's degree in physics. He was planning to enroll in a master's degree program in England when he received news that his father had died. Because his family was having financial problems, he felt compelled to go back to Mauritius to help his family.

Rajesh increased his devotion to his Hindu prayers after the death of his father. He prayed every day, often with a sense of anger and bitterness. "I always prayed: 'Why am I in such a situation?'" he said. At that time, work was hard to find in Mauritius. Rajesh had heard that Italy was not as strict as some other countries with work visas at the time, so he immigrated there to find work in the mid-1980s. After more than a decade of living and working in Italy, Rajesh was employed by the Acutis family in December 1995 to help take care of Carlo. "And I met Carlo, such a small child", Rajesh remembers.

After Carlo made his First Communion at the age of seven, Rajesh would walk with Carlo to the church around the corner from his house for Mass or to pray on his way to and from school. "He used to wake up early to attend the Mass in the morning before going to school. Then, after Mass, he used to stay a little bit longer in front of the tabernacle. If there was no Mass, he would stay there [at the church], and then I would take him to school. That was my job", Rajesh said.

Rajesh observed how young Carlo's behavior changed when he entered a church. While Carlo prayed in front of the tabernacle, Rajesh would quietly sit in the back and watch the young boy as he prayed earnestly. "His behavior changed when he was inside the church, with all respect. He knew that there was something different where Jesus lives. . . . That touched my heart . . . when I saw Carlo's behavior", he said.

Carlo was eager to talk to Rajesh about the things that he loved: heaven, the Mass, and the presence of Jesus in the Eucharist. He explained everything with "such a sweetness", Rajesh said. "He talked always about the Eucharist, Jesus, how he suffered for us . . . sacrificed his life for us", Rajesh said. "Carlo, he told me that . . . wherever you go, you may find Jesus present in Flesh, Soul, and Blood [in the tabernacle]."

Rajesh also observed Carlo's care and concern for others. He said that young Carlo once gathered up his toys, including some nice Christmas presents from his grandparents and parents, and asked Rajesh to accompany him to the park to sell his toys to give the money to the poor. "He collected the money, and there were some poor people lying there in front of the church. They were sleeping on the floor during winter. It was quite cold. . . . He said that they were suffering, you know. They needed help", Rajesh said. "When I saw Carlo's acts, you know, of such a small child, then I got converted."

Carlo helped Rajesh learn how to pray the Rosary and invited him to pray it together with him and his parents. "He had formed the habit . . . of reciting the Holy Rosary every night before going to bed", Rajesh remembers. Carlo told Rajesh that a person can pray the Rosary without being baptized, but only practicing Catholics can receive the Holy Eucharist. Carlo explained that the Eucharist is the culmination of charity and that the virtues are acquired through a sacramental life.[1] Rajesh remembers that Carlo quoted from memory some of the passages of Jesus' Bread of Life discourse from the Gospel of John.[2] "He knew the *Catechism of the Catholic Church* almost by heart and explained it so brilliantly that he managed to excite me about the importance of the sacraments", Rajesh said.[3]

"So, slowly, slowly . . . he used to tell me the importance of Baptism and so many other things also", he added.[4] "All those experiences changed my life. And I could see the living God."

Rajesh Is Baptized

Four years after first meeting Carlo, Rajesh was baptized. He was in his late thirties at the time, and as an adult entering the Catholic Church, he received at once all the Catholic sacraments of initiation: Baptism, First Communion, and Confirmation. Making this ceremony in 1999 extra sweet for eight-year-old Carlo, the Mass was offered in his parish of Santa Maria Segreta. As even a young child, Carlo was already sharing Mary's "secret".

The Acutis family threw a party afterward for Rajesh and his friends, sharing sweets and snacks at their apartment. Rajesh let Carlo pick where to go out for dinner. He said that Carlo proposed: "Let's go to the Chinese restaurant today because it's a special day." Rajesh joked in reply: "It's special for me, but it's more special for you because you like Chinese food." Joking aside, Carlo later told his parents: "There are many people who do not realize what an infinite gift it is to receive Baptism."[5]

After his Baptism and First Communion, Rajesh joined Carlo in attending daily Mass, but as a full participant in Communion, rather than as an observer. "I took the opportunity to be with Carlo to learn more and more and to . . . attend the Mass", he said.

Rajesh's Family

Rajesh's niece Vanessa became friends with Carlo, though she was four years older than he. When Vanessa was upset about her parents' separation, Carlo told her: "You cannot see God. But he sees you, and he knows how much you suffer. He protects you, and he will always be beside you to protect you. And he will give you signs to let you know that he is there."[6] Carlo then gave her a Bible so that she could know God and know how much he loved her. "God is there for everyone", Carlo told her. "If you open your heart to him, he will show you the way."[7]

Vanessa remembers: "Carlo talked about God as if he was utterly beautiful. I remember that he told me that he wanted to be bright and radiant like Jesus, and if we all put into practice the teachings of Jesus, we would all be more beautiful and radiant."[8] Vanessa also witnessed how Carlo was both detached and generous with his toys and possessions. She recalled that Carlo gave her some of his toys because she did not have as many as he did. "He was very happy and gave them to me with ease", Vanessa said. "There was never any act of superiority on his part or humiliation on mine. . . . He was a true friend of mine. He was a very simple guy, who did not demand anything, even though he could afford everything."[9]

Rajesh's mother came to visit her son in Milan a few years after his Baptism and stayed with him and the Acutis family for three months. She wore her traditional Mauritian sari and sometimes accompanied Rajesh to pick up Carlo from school. Some of the students at Carlo's school began laughing and making fun of "the Indian lady" in strange clothes. Carlo heard their teasing remarks, and rather than joining in or being embarrassed, as many kids his age would have been tempted to do, he approached the kids who were making jokes and calmly said: "Please, have respect. She is Rajesh's mom, and she's a very kind lady."

Rajesh was impressed by Carlo's maturity in this situation, but he was not surprised because he had seen firsthand Carlo's openness to people from different cultures. As an immigrant in Italy, Rajesh had friends from the Philippines, Bangladesh, Sri Lanka, and Morocco as well as other African countries. He said: "Carlo, whenever he used to come across those people [i.e., immigrants], he used to be so friendly. Even with my friends, he used to ask so many questions and talk to them . . . as if they were no different."

Carlo invited Rajesh's mom to come with them to Mass; she said afterward that she did not understand anything. Besides having little familiarity with the Catholic faith, Rajesh's mom did not speak Italian, so Carlo would speak with her in English. He would sit in the kitchen with Rajesh's mother and tell her in English about Jesus and the Catholic faith. He told her the story of the apparition of the Virgin Mary in Lourdes, France, in such a compelling way that she wanted to visit the pilgrimage site. With the help of the

Acutis family, Rajesh's mother stayed in Lourdes for a week. When she returned to Mauritius, she asked to be baptized.

After her Baptism, Rajesh's mother visited the sick in Mauritius and prayed with them, using some of the holy water from Lourdes. "That was Carlo's magic", Rajesh said. "He could convert me and my mom too."

6

Information Superhighway

The first nine years of Carlo's life saw a rapid technological explosion that had already begun to transform society. Amazon, Yahoo, eBay, Internet Explorer, and Windows 95 had all been launched by the time Carlo was five. Google was founded when he was seven. The term "information superhighway" became synonymous with the Internet in the 1990s. Stocks for many new Internet companies boomed for two years in the late '90s, and possibilities with online technology seemed virtually infinite. Computer technology also had its upheavals at the turn of the millennium—fear of Y2K gripped the world: Would the switch to a four-digit format for years cause critical malfunctions in electronic infrastructures all over the globe?* Then the "dot-com bubble" burst—but there was no stopping the information superhighway.

Carlo was eight years old when Pope John Paul II inaugurated the Great Jubilee for the new millennium. The Acutis family was able to get tickets to be present in Saint Peter's Square when John Paul II made an act of entrustment of the world and the new millennium to the Immaculate Heart of Mary on October 8, 2000.[1] Carlo and his family (including his cousin Umberto and his aunt and uncle from Rome)

* Previously, in some computer applications, years were truncated to the final two digits. Beginning with the year 2000, all four digits would be required to differentiate the century.

joined the pope and the large crowd of people gathered within the "arms" of Bernini's colonnade in praying for the Virgin Mary's intercession for the new millennium. Carlo's mother could tell that her son was impressed by the scene in Saint Peter's Square as so many people prayed together in unity with the pope in front of the statue of Our Lady of Fátima brought from Portugal.[2]

During the act of entrustment, Saint John Paul II asked for the intercession of the Blessed Virgin Mary. He prayed:

> The Church today, through the voice of the Successor of Peter, in union with so many Pastors assembled here from every corner of the world, seeks refuge in your motherly protection and trustingly begs your intercession as she faces the challenges which lie hidden in the future. . . .
>
> Today we wish to entrust to you the future that awaits us, and we ask you to be with us on our way. We are the men and women of an extraordinary time, exhilarating yet full of contradictions.

The Polish pope warned, "Humanity now has instruments of unprecedented power. . . . Today as never before in the past, humanity stands at a crossroads."[3]

Coding Kid

It was around the year 2000 when Carlo received his first computer as a gift.[4] He had expressed his love for computers years earlier. Antonia remembers that, at six years old, Carlo would "go around the house saying, 'I am a computer scientist.'"[5]

It is easy to imagine the boy eagerly listening to the rhythmic tones that played as the dial-up modem connected to the Web through phone lines at what would seem today like a turtle's pace. The inner workings of the computer captivated Carlo's imagination, and he begged his mother for books on how to code. Carlo's mother bought him a computer programming textbook at the Polytechnic University of Milan bookstore. Using the book, Carlo studied C and C++, some of the most widely used programming languages at the time. Those languages were required knowledge for many information technology (IT) professionals.[6]

Carlo was a self-starter. Within a few years, he had taught himself other programming languages too, including Java, according to his mother.[7] He had a large stack of books on computer coding, which, for a time, were stored in the Archdiocese of Milan's Office for the Causes of Saints.[8] Carlo's uncle, whose work focused on computers, gave him computer software to tinker with, including the Adobe Suite and Maya for 3D editing.[9] "He taught himself everything, including 3D animation", his mother said. "It was unbelievable."[10] A friend of the Acutis family who worked in the technology field told Carlo's postulator: "Carlo Acutis was a child who had such skill in computer programming that it almost baffled me because I wondered how a boy of that age could talk about computers with such ability, similar to my own. I wrote several books for publishers who specialized in the publication of computer science texts used by college students and professionals."[11]

When Carlo was eleven in 2002, surfing the Web, for most young people, meant sitting at home in front of a desktop computer.[12] Although some flip phones could connect to the web, typing on a cell phone necessitated hitting the same button multiple times to select the right letter.[13] Carlo had multiple laptops over the years, but he spent most of his time at the desk in his bedroom, using a desktop computer, which Rajesh affectionately referred to as Carlo's "Big Mac".[14]

After school, Carlo would sometimes teach his friend Vanessa how to master the computer. She said that Carlo told her, "To really know how to use the computer, you must also be able to code. . . . Otherwise you are just a user and not a programmer."[15] Carlo also volunteered to help a religious community, the Little Sisters of the Lamb, with a problem that the sisters had with their computer. Sister Mariana Martin recalls: "We had mentioned the fact that we had a problem with our computer. He took his and began to look for a solution. Five minutes later, he gave me the answer, and I was able to solve the problem we had been having for months."[16]

Carlo's grandmother Luana noted how Carlo used the Internet to seek out opportunities to go to Mass: "On our travels, as soon as we arrived in a foreign place, he would search on the Internet for where there was a church and the times of Mass, so as not to miss it. He was so keen on it."[17]

Video Games

Like many boys his age in the early 2000s, Carlo was very interested in video games. His mother recalls that he liked Nintendo Game Boy, and GameCube* as well as PlayStation and Xbox.[18] Rajesh remembers that Carlo started playing video games around the age of eight and particularly liked video games that involved race cars.[19]

Carlos' friend Federico Oldani has memories of playing Halo with him.[20] Halo was a first-person shooter Xbox

* For Christmas one year, Carlo received a GameCube.

game. Its release by Microsoft in 2001 was one of the most successful video game releases in history, selling more than five million copies. The game's continued success over the years also sparked a conversation about "video game addiction", which the World Health Organization has formally recognized as an illness.[21]

Eventually, Carlo's parents imposed a rule that he could not play video games for more than two hours a week.[22] His mother says that this helped him to grow in the virtue of temperance because he learned how to enjoy recreation in a balanced way without becoming so engrossed in video games that he lost sense of his priorities.

With advances in high-speed Internet and live online multiplayer gaming, young people today face a steeper battle if they want to rein in the hours they spend playing video games. One young gamer in 2017 expressed frustration that his parents did not understand, telling a researcher: "With Xbox whenever you play online with people, you can't pause your game. Well, when your parents want something from you, they demand it then and now. And when you try to tell them, 'I'm playing online with other people,' I can't just pause and hop to it, they don't understand."[23]

For Carlo, playing video games with friends was still integrated with his life of faith. He had conversations with his gaming buddies about the importance of going to Mass and Confession.[24] Mattia, a boy who often played video games with Carlo, testified to the Vatican: "There was a time when I thought he was going to Mass at his mother's behest; then I understood, and I became more and more convinced that it was his personal choice, something he wanted to do freely and from his heart."[25]

7

In the Footsteps of Saint Francis

In 2000, Carlo's parents bought a vacation home in Assisi, a hill town in the central Italian region of Umbria.[1] The town was made famous by Saint Francis of Assisi, the thirteenth-century son of a silk merchant who rejected his former life of extravagance for a life of poverty and complete dedication to God as a "lesser brother".

Saint Francis and his friars took the Middle Ages by storm. The "Little Poor Man of Assisi" became the most popular saint of his time.[2] His hometown has been a place of pilgrimage since his death in October 1226. Because of this, Assisi retains its medieval character and has become a town saturated by the Catholic faith.

With their new second home, the Acutis family began to visit Assisi for Christmas, Easter, and summer holidays. The tranquility and natural beauty of the Umbrian olive trees, grapevines, and farmhouses that make up Assisi's expansive vistas were a far cry from the noise and bustle of the city streets of Milan, where Carlo grew up. Instead of fashionistas strolling down the avenues, habited religious walked Assisi's cobblestone streets.

"Carlo had a special bond with Assisi. He had Assisi in his heart. He said it was the city where he felt happiest", his mother recalls.[3]

Italians call Umbria "il Cuore Verde d'Italia", or "the

Green Heart of Italy". Carlo enjoyed hiking and going on nature walks in the fresh air with his dogs on the hill town's tree-lined slopes.* The familiar photo of Carlo sporting a red polo shirt with a blue collar and wearing a backpack—now shared thousands of times on the Internet—was likely taken on top of Assisi's Mount Subasio.[4] Another widely shared photo of Carlo (wearing the same red shirt but without the backpack) was taken in front of an Umbrian hillside in a meadow in Castelluccio,[5] where hundreds of pine trees have been planted on a hillside in the shape of the map of Italy.[6]

During his hikes in the Umbrian hills, Carlo would make little crosses out of the sticks and pieces of wood that he found along the path. He told his mother that he imagined that someone finding them would remember Jesus crucified out of love for mankind.[7] Carlo would also sometimes go on walks wearing gloves to pick up litter and trash along the hiking trail.[8]

Carlo relished the spiritual nourishment that the town of Assisi provided, and he attended Mass and eucharistic adoration in the town's many churches. One resident of Assisi told Carlo's postulator: "I go to Mass every day, and I met Carlo at Mass every day when he was in Assisi. I remember with a deep impression the great faith and his tender and angelic smile. In Carlo, a great purity of heart shone through."[9] Carlo's mother has said that a nun in Assisi once approached her and told her that her son had a special mission in the Church.[10] After Carlo's death, a Franciscan friar who served at the Basilica of Saint Clare remembered:

* One of the Acutis family dogs was named after the second most famous saint from Assisi, Saint Clare, in Italian, "Chiara".

"Several times I saw him at the basilica when I was serving. He always came to Mass. And for a twelve- or thirteen-year-old boy, that was unusual."[11]

Carlo and his mother went on a long spiritual retreat together at the Franciscan Sanctuary of La Verna, about seventy miles north of Assisi, during his summer break.* The sanctuary is a place of pilgrimage, built on the spot where Saint Francis is said to have received the stigmata (the wounds that Jesus received on his hands and feet during his Crucifixion) on September 14, 1224.

The summers in Assisi exposed Carlo to the spiritualities of several religious orders. Among them were the Little Sisters of the Lamb, who wore blue habits and would go from door to door asking for bread "so that all, rich and poor alike, might receive the Light of the Gospel: Jesus, the Lamb of God".[12] When the Little Sisters knocked on the door of the Acutis family home in Assisi on a hot August day, Carlo answered and told them: "I will call my father, who is in charge of these things."[13] Carlo's father later testified to the Vatican: "Carlo not only wanted to give them bread, but he asked me to invite them to lunch, and I granted his wish."[14] Sister Mariana Martin, one of the Little Sisters who shared the lunch with Carlo, later commented that what struck her about the boy was "his ability to listen" and "his joy and his peace in conversing and explaining things".[15]

Carlo also befriended some of the cloistered Poor Clare nuns in Spello, another Umbrian hill town near Assisi. One of the nuns taught him this prayer, which he began to repeat regularly: "Wounds of Jesus, founts of love and mercy

* Carlo's mother said that it was on this retreat in La Verna that Carlo meditated more deeply on the Passion of Christ and was inspired to make the crosses out of sticks on their nature walks. Salzano Acutis and Rodari, *Il segreto*, 280–81.

for us, speak of us to the Divine Father and obtain for us an inner transformation."[16] Another Poor Clare nun, Sister Luigina Consoli, remembers that ten-year-old Carlo asked her to "pray a lot for sinners" because "among my friends are those who are far from Jesus".[17]

The Porziuncola and Purgatory

One of Carlo's favorite spots to pray in Assisi was the Porziuncola, the place where Saint Francis founded the Order of Friars Minor in 1209, entrusting it to the protection of the Blessed Virgin Mary. G.K. Chesterton wrote that the Porziuncola became "the home of many homeless men".[18] It is also the location where Saint Clare received her religious habit from Francis and founded the Poor Clares.

Today the Porziuncola is a church within a church. The small brick fourth-century building, which measures about eighteen feet by ten feet, is inside the massive Basilica of Saint Mary of the Angels in the valley below Assisi's historic hill town. The Porziuncola was one of the places in Assisi that Carlo sought out to pray for sinners and for the souls in purgatory, according to his mother. "He prayed a lot for sinners, for their salvation. He was always making sacrifices—saying no to desserts, no to video games or films", Antonia remembers.[19] "He had a great devotion to the souls in purgatory. He liked to pray and apply indulgences to them."

The Porziuncola Indulgence has been tied to this church for centuries. According to the *Catechism of the Catholic Church*, an indulgence is "the remission . . . of the temporal punishment due to sin whose guilt has already been forgiven".[20] Originally the Porziuncola Indulgence could be obtained only by praying inside the Porziuncola church itself. In 1967, Pope Paul VI extended the Porziuncola Indulgence in *Indulgentiarum doctrina*, making it possible to obtain the plenary indulgence in any Catholic parish church on August 2.[21] To receive the indulgence, a person must meet the usual requirements—that is, he must be in the state of grace and have no attachment to sin; he must pray an Our Father and recite the Creed for the intentions of the pope; and he must receive the Eucharist and sacramental Confession within twenty days before or after the act of prayer.[22]

Carlo's grandmother Luana remembers that Carlo often offered Masses, prayers, and periods of eucharistic adoration for the souls in purgatory.[23] His devotions included the Divine Mercy Novena, prayed in preparation for Divine Mercy Sunday, a feast instituted by Pope John Paul II in 2000. Carlo asked his parents to pray this novena by Saint Faustina with him in the nine days before the feast,[24] and Luana recalls that her grandson asked her to pray the novena twice.[25] According to his postulator, "Carlo was convinced that it was very difficult not to end up in [purgatory]."[26] Carlo used the writings of Saint Faustina Kowalska and Saint Catherine of Genoa, who wrote a treatise on purgatory, to convince others of the reality of purgatory and hell, and even debated a priest who denied their existence.[27]

Carlo and Francis

Domenico Sorrentino was installed as bishop of Assisi and its neighboring areas in February 2006, when Carlo was fourteen. The bishop has written a short book in Italian titled *Originali, non fotocopie: Carlo Acutis e Francesco d'Assisi* (Originals, not photocopies: Carlo Acutis and Francis of Assisi) that outlines some of the similarities he sees between Carlo and Francis, even though the two lived more than seven centuries apart. The bishop posits that both came from wealthy families and rejected the usual path of people of their status for a radical adherence to the gospel and a particular closeness to Christ in the poor and in the Eucharist.

Although Sorrentino never met Carlo in person—Carlo died several months after the bishop's installation—he says that by the time he arrived in Assisi, Carlo had already left an indelible mark on the town.[28] The bishop said that he had to discover Carlo "little by little from the memories of the people of Assisi".

"In the prolonged stays that he and his family made in the 'City of the Poverello,'* a special connection was established", he said.[29] "There is the shopkeeper who remembers him shopping with his mother. There are his friends who remember him while he was swimming in the pool." It is a fitting coincidence that the time from Saint Francis' feast day, October 4, to the day Carlo died, October 12, is nine days, the length of a novena. "Assisi was the place where Carlo's soul flew to unexplored heights", Carlo's mother said.[30]

* *Poverello* means "poor man", referring to Saint Francis.

8

Carlo on Pilgrimage: Eucharistic Miracles

Every summer since 1980, Catholics have gathered in Rimini, a seaside town on Italy's Adriatic coast, for a weeklong event organized by the Catholic movement Communion and Liberation. One distinctive feature of this "meeting for friendship among peoples", more commonly known simply as the Rimini Meeting, is that it hosts several exhibitions in which hundreds of thousands of visitors can walk through exhibition halls and read informative panels accompanied by photographs on topics from art and literature to science and history in order to facilitate contemplation of "what is true, good, and beautiful".[1]

In the summer of 2002, eleven-year-old Carlo tagged along with his mother as she traveled to Rimini for this meeting at the end of August.* Antonia was a speaker on a panel at the Rimini Meeting that year and was listed in the program as a representative of the San Clemente Institute.[2] Carlo's mother shared how she had founded the institute two years earlier with the mission of spreading "the fundamental truths of our faith: the existence of God, the divinity of Jesus, and the presence of Jesus in the Eucharist".[3]

Though Carlo's mother had not attended weekly Mass before Carlo was born, the spark ignited by her young son's

* According to Communion and Liberation, Carlo was the first "Blessed" in the Church to have participated in the Rimini Meeting as a visitor.

enthusiasm for God had led Antonia to become an energetic and entrepreneurial catechist in her own right. By the time Carlo was nine, Antonia had also joined the Vatican's Pontifical Academy Cultorum Martyrum—an academy established by the Holy See to advance the devotion to early Christian saints and martyrs—in addition to organizing conferences and lectures on Catholic topics for the San Clemente Institute.*

At the Rimini Meeting, Antonia spoke on a panel that was presenting a new book that she had contributed to: *Piccolo catechismo eucaristico* (Little eucharistic catechism). Carlo's understanding of the Real Presence of Christ in the Eucharist was formed,[4] in part, by this eucharistic catechism book. The book explains the following, for instance:

> The priest does not say, "This is the body of Jesus", but he says, "This is my body"; he does not say, "This is the blood of Jesus", but he says, "This is my blood." This means that the one who speaks these words is actually Jesus. It is Jesus who consecrates the bread and the wine with the help of the priest, who, as it were, lends Jesus his voice and his hands.[5]

The "little eucharistic catechism" included sections on eucharistic miracles and short biographies of saints who were particularly devoted to the Eucharist. According to his mother, Carlo helped with the creation of the catechism by using a graphics program on his computer to develop images to accompany the text.[6]

The theme of the Rimini Meeting that Carlo attended in 2002 was "The feeling of things, the contemplation of

* The institute organized conferences in Rome and at the Vatican in 2001 in collaboration with the Pontifical Oriental Institute to mark the nineteenth centenary of the martyrdom of Saint Clement, the organization's namesake.

beauty". It included exhibitions on the life of Saint Joseph Moscati, the Modena Cathedral, and the physics behind waves.[7] After viewing the exhibitions and hearing his mother discuss the Eucharist on the panel, Carlo was inspired to create an exhibition on eucharistic miracles.[8]

Over the next two and a half years, Carlo and his family worked to create panels describing the history behind eucharistic miracles for the exhibition.[9] With his Internet savvy and his language skills, Carlo was able to find images and to research information on different miracles.[10] One can imagine Carlo, as he entered his teenage years, sitting at the desk by his bedroom window for hours, searching on Google for facts from the history behind a fourteenth-century miracle in France to a modern scientific analysis of the blood sample on a transubstantiated eucharistic host.[11] Rajesh remembers that Carlo would do his research on eucharistic miracles at night while listening to classical music after finishing his homework and praying the Rosary with his family. Carlo would meet Rajesh in the kitchen for a late-night snack and tell him: "Rajesh, I have to leave you now because I have so many things to do."[12]

Carlo asked his parents if his family could make pilgrimages to some of the sites of eucharistic miracles during their vacations in Italy, France, Spain, and Portugal. The boy was eager to tell others about eucharistic miracles that occurred in distant countries such as India and Peru and how God had made his presence known on far-off continents that he would never see in his lifetime.[13] Little did Carlo know at the time that the exhibition itself would go on to traverse the planet.*

* According to the website linked to the exhibition, as of the beginning of 2023, the eucharistic miracles display has been hosted on all five continents,

Eucharistic Miracle Sites Documented by Carlo

Following are some of the eucharistic miracle locations included in the exhibition that Carlo had a personal connection to during his lifetime.

Florence, Italy (1230, 1595)

When Carlo was seven years old, he was exposed to the concept of a eucharistic miracle during a trip with his mother and grandmother to Tuscany. During their visit to the cities of Florence, Pisa, and Lucca, the family stayed with some religious sisters at the Church of Saint Ambrose in Florence. The church is believed to be the site of two eucharistic miracles. The first took place in 1230. A priest unintentionally left some consecrated wine in the chalice after Mass and returned the next day to find coagulated blood.[14] The bishop had the blood from the chalice brought to him in a reliquary. He kept it for several weeks before returning it to the religious sisters, who have kept the reliquary for veneration in the Church of Saint Ambrose to this day.[15]

The second recorded miracle occurred on Good Friday in 1595 when a fire broke out in the church. In the commotion caused by the fire, there was an attempt to save the Blessed Sacrament kept in the tabernacle, but six consecrated hosts fell onto the ground. After the fire, the hosts were found intact and joined together. Archbishop Marzio Medici of Florence examined the hosts thirty years later and found them to be incorrupt. He had them placed in a reliquary that is displayed, together with the thirteenth-century reliquary, each year in May for public veneration.

---

in nearly ten thousand parishes in the United States alone, and at the Marian shrines of Fátima, Lourdes, and Guadalupe. "Panel A".

During the Tuscany trip, Carlo also visited the tomb of Saint Zita in the Basilica of San Frediano in Lucca, Italy. The thirteenth-century saint who, from the age of twelve, worked as a servant in a household, would wake up early to attend Mass. When Carlo prayed at her tomb, he asked Saint Zita for the grace to help him to build a special relationship with his guardian angel.[16]

Lourdes, France (1888)

When Carlo was thirteen, he prayed in a holy grotto in France where the Virgin Mary had appeared to a poor girl of about the same age in 1858. Saint Bernadette Soubirous was only fourteen years old when the Blessed Virgin Mary revealed herself at Lourdes as the Immaculate Conception and instructed her to dig in the ground and drink from a spring that appeared. Ever since Bernadette's act of humble obedience, millions of pilgrims have come to the Lourdes grotto to wash in the water from the spring, where medically verified healings have occurred through the intercession of Our Lady of Lourdes.*

Less well known are the eucharistic healings that have been documented in Lourdes and are showcased in the Acutis family's eucharistic miracles exhibition. The first eucharistic healing occurred in 1888. With more and more pilgrims coming to the French town each year after the Marian apparition, a priest in the pilgrimage office proposed having a eucharistic procession. During the first procession with

* According to the Lourdes Shrine, there have been seventy medically verified miracles recognized by the Church at Lourdes and many more cases of healing reported to the shrine (more than seven thousand) since the apparitions. "The Miracles of Lourdes", Lourdes Sanctuaire, https://www.lourdes-france.org/en/the-miracles-of-lourdes/.

the Blessed Sacrament on August 22, 1888, Pietro Delanoy, a man with ataxia, a degenerative disease of the nervous system, was instantly healed when the monstrance passed by him during the procession. This was the first of many healings that would occur in Lourdes involving the Eucharist. Marie Bigot, a deaf and partially blind woman, recovered her hearing and eyesight during a eucharistic procession. Louise Jamain was cured of pulmonary and intestinal tuberculosis. Alice Couteaul was cured of multiple sclerosis.

During the 2005 trip to Lourdes, thirteen-year-old Carlo made a promise to Our Lady to be more faithful to praying the Rosary and consecrated himself to the Immaculate Heart of Mary.[17] Carlo remained absorbed in prayer in Lourdes for more than an hour, his mother recalls.[18] He also bought some statuettes of the Virgin Mary that he filled with Lourdes water to give as gifts, and his mother loaded in the trunk of their car ten liters of water from the spring in the Grotto of Massabielle. Carlo's first rosary, given to him by a relative, had been a rosary from Lourdes, and he carried it with him during his travels.[19]

Lanciano, Italy (Eighth Century)

"Carlo always mentioned one miracle in particular", his mother recalls—Lanciano.[20] The central Italian town is the site of one of the oldest and most well-known eucharistic miracles in the world. The transformed eucharistic host has been the subject of multiple scientific analyses.

Tradition holds that the Lanciano miracle occurred sometime between A.D. 700 and 750 in the monastery church of Saint Legonziano. Though the ancient historical documentation was lost over the centuries, a manuscript from 1631 laid out an account of what happened according to the local oral history at the time:

> A monk who, not very steadfast in his faith, well educated in the sciences of the world, but ignorant in God's ones, lived day by day doubting the true Body of Christ was in the consecrated host and likewise if the true blood was in the wine. . . . One morning, in the midst of his Sacrifice [of the Mass], after uttering the most sacred words of consecration . . . he saw . . . the Bread turned into Flesh and the Wine turned into Blood.[21]

The monk then told the congregation: "O fortunate witnesses, to whom the Blessed God, to confound my unbelief, has wished to reveal Himself visible to our eyes! Come, brethren, and marvel at our God, so close to us. Behold the flesh and blood of our Most Beloved Christ."[22] The transformed host and five solid fragments of clotted blood were kept for centuries in a silver monstrance in the church, which eventually came under the custody of the Franciscan Order.

According to his spiritual director, Carlo particularly liked to tell people about the Lanciano miracle because of the scientific analyses that were conducted on the centuries-old host.* The most extensive scientific examinations were carried out in 1970–1971 by Italian medical professor Dr. Odoardo Linoli with the assistance of Dr. Ruggero Bertelli.[23] Linoli took two small samples from the host (a total of twenty milligrams of tissue) and a small fragment from the clotted blood to study over the course of one hundred days.

* Both Carlo's mother and his spiritual director testified that Carlo especially liked the Lanciano miracle. Carlo told his spiritual director that he brought up the miracle of Lanciano when he wanted to "persuade some people who did not attend Sunday Mass" that Jesus is present in the Eucharist.

Dr. Franco Serafini, an American cardiologist, has described Dr. Linoli's final report as "incredibly detailed". The investigation found that the sample from the transformed host was human heart muscle and that the blood belonged to the AB group (the same blood type documented on the Shroud of Turin). Linoli further concluded that the specimens would have rapidly undergone a process of decay if they had originally come from a corpse and that no evidence of preservative substances was found in the samples.[24]

Dr. Linoli participated in the congress on eucharistic miracles in Rome at the Pontifical Athenaeum Regina Apostolorum that featured the Acutis family's eucharistic miracles exhibition in May 2005.[25] More than thirty years after his study of the Lanciano miracle was first published, Linoli reflected: "There is no doubt at all that it is cardiac tissue."[26]

Girona, Spain (1297)

While on a family trip to Valencia, Spain, the Acutis family drove some three hundred miles to spend the night in the small town of Girona. The Spanish town had been the site of a eucharistic miracle in 1297, and Carlo wanted to take photos for the eucharistic miracles exhibition.

According to the local tradition, a priest who offered Mass at a convent of Benedictine nuns was shocked when he could not swallow the consecrated Host. After he removed it from his mouth and placed it in a corporal, the priest and the nuns were amazed to see that the cloth contained what appeared to be a piece of flesh, dripping with blood.[27] The priest confessed that he had been doubting the Real Presence of Jesus in the Eucharist when he felt the host grow inside his mouth.

The host and the corporal were placed in a reliquary monstrance in the Cathedral of Girona; unfortunately, both were destroyed during the Spanish Civil War in 1936. Nevertheless, Carlo still wanted to visit the site where the miracle occurred and take photos of the church for the exhibition.[28] On the way to Girona, the Acutis family stopped in Barcelona, where Carlo asked to go to Mass at the Barcelona Cathedral, a medieval gothic cathedral dedicated to the Holy Cross and Saint Eulalia.[29]

Assisi, Italy (1240)

The Acutis family—no doubt influenced by their time spent living in Saint Francis' hometown—decided to include in the exhibition's panels the eucharistic miracle of Saint Clare of Assisi. The thirteenth-century founder of the Poor Clares, the first female branch of the Franciscan Order, was known for her devotion to the Eucharist and her vow of poverty.

In 1240, Saint Clare, using the Blessed Sacrament, courageously sought to protect the city of Assisi from an attack of Saracen soldiers. Thomas of Celano's book *The Life of Saint Clare, Virgin* describes Clare as possessing "unflinching courage" as she asked to be led to the enemy with a silver and ivory case containing the Blessed Sacrament:

> And prostrate in prayer before the Lord, she spoke in tears to her Christ: "Behold, my Lord, does it please you to hand over to the pagans your servants, whom I have trained in your love? I pray you, Lord, preserve these your handmaids whom I cannot now save by myself."[30]

Saint Clare heard a voice respond: "I will always protect you." And she replied, "My Lord . . . if it is your wish, protect also this city which is sustained by your love."

According to Celano, the Saracens fled after seeing the "power of Clare's prayer", and Clare commanded the sisters in her order to tell no one about what had happened while she was still alive. Clare's bravery has been depicted in many paintings after her death. In Catholic art, the saint has been depicted holding a monstrance containing the Blessed Sacrament high above her head as the attacking soldiers are struck back by the light radiating from the host.

While his family was in Assisi, Carlo would sometimes attend Mass at the Basilica of Saint Clare, where he could pray before the San Damiano crucifix that had spoken to Saint Francis and at the tomb of Saint Clare in the crypt chapel of the basilica.

Fátima, Portugal (1916)

Carlo went on a pilgrimage to Fátima with his family in February 2006, when he was fourteen. The Acutis family prepared for their pilgrimage by reading the diary of Lucia de Jesus Rosa dos Santos,* the eldest of three children in rural Portugal who received apparitions of the Blessed Virgin Mary. The diary made a deep impression on Carlo.[31]

While climbing the hill to the Loca do Cabeço in Fátima,[32] Carlo was well-aware of the miraculous events that occurred there, as his family had included the story in the eucharistic miracles exhibition that had premiered the previous year. At the Loca do Cabeço, Lucia and two other children, Jacinta and Francisco Marto, were visited by an angel three times before they received apparitions of Our Lady of Fátima in 1917. The angel said: "Do not be afraid. I am the Angel of

* Sister Lucia died in February 2005, one year before Carlo made his pilgrimage to Fátima.

Peace. Pray with me: My God, I believe, I adore, I hope, and I love you. I ask pardon for those who do not believe, do not adore, do not hope, and do not love you."

During his third apparition, in the fall of 1916, the angel gave Lucia Holy Communion miraculously. Lucia recorded the event in her memoir:

> We lifted our heads to see what was happening. The Angel was holding in his left hand a chalice and over it, in the air, was a host from which drops of blood fell into the chalice. The Angel leaves the chalice in the air, kneels near us, and tells us to repeat three times:
>
> "Most Holy Trinity, Father, Son, and Holy Spirit, I adore You profoundly, and I offer You the Most Precious Body, Blood, Soul, and Divinity of Jesus Christ, present in all the tabernacles of the world, in reparation for the outrages, sacrileges, and indifferences by which He is offended. And by the infinite merits of His most Sacred Heart and the Immaculate Heart of Mary, I beg the conversion of poor sinners."
>
> After that, he rose and took again in his hand the chalice and the host. The host he gave to me and the contents of the chalice he gave to Jacinta and Francisco, saying at the same time: "Eat and drink the Body and Blood of Jesus Christ terribly outraged by the ingratitude of men. Offer reparation for their sakes and console God."[33]

Carlo told his spiritual director that he liked to tell people about the angel's message to the shepherd children in Fátima in hope of encouraging them to attend Sunday Mass.[34]

Two religious sisters, Sister Maria João Marquès Antes and Sister Angela Codeluppilo, showed Carlo's family around Fátima and told them all about the apparitions, including when the three shepherd children asked Our Lady whether they would be taken to heaven.[35] Carlo expressed concern when he learned that Our Lady of Fátima told Lucia and Jacinta that they would be taken to heaven but warned little Francisco that he would have to recite many Rosaries to get to heaven.[36] He asked his parents: "If Francisco, who was so good, so kind, and so simple, had to recite so many Rosaries to get into heaven, how can I deserve it, I who in comparison with him am so much less holy?"[37] According to his postulator, Carlo was particularly moved by the Fátima children's small sacrifices, and he attempted to imitate them by giving up Nutella or refraining from watching television in an effort to offer up what he called "a bouquet of roses to Mary that she will use to help her children most in need".[38] Carlo also kept the Five First Saturdays Devotion requested by the Virgin Mary in her words to Lucia.*

Santarém, Portugal (1247)

While in Portugal on the pilgrimage to Fátima, Carlo and his family were able to visit the Church of the Holy Miracle in the town of Santarém, about a forty-minute drive south of Fátima.

According to local tradition, a woman in Santarém in the thirteenth century was convinced that her husband was being unfaithful to her and consulted a sorceress who practiced black magic. The sorceress promised to make the woman's

* The devotion involves receiving Communion, saying five decades of the Rosary, and keeping Mary company with fifteen minutes of prayerful meditation on the mysteries of the Rosary on the first Saturday of the month for five consecutive months as an act of reparation to the Immaculate Heart of Mary. One should also receive sacramental Confession within eight days before or after the first Saturday.

husband love her again in exchange for a stolen consecrated eucharistic host.

Consumed with jealousy, the woman obeyed the witch, and after receiving Communion at her parish, the Church of Saint Stephen, she hid the host in her veil. On her way back from the church, the host in the veil started to bleed. In a panic, the woman placed the veil and the host in a chest in her bedroom. That night, rays of bright light shone through the chest. The woman and her husband awoke to find angels adoring the bleeding host. The wife then told her husband all that had happened, and the two spent the night in prayer before the host before going to inform the priest what had occurred. In a solemn procession, the priest returned the host to the church, where the Eucharist continued to bleed for three days. After an episcopal investigation, the miraculous host was placed it in a gold and silver reliquary, where the host is still enthroned today.[39]

Many have made pilgrimages to the Santarém church over the centuries. Saint Elizabeth of Portugal made a pilgrimage to pray before the miraculous host in 1322, as did Saint Francis Xavier before he set out on a mission to India.

The Acutis family's pilgrimage in 2006 coincided with the church's celebration of the 750th anniversary of the eucharistic miracle in Santarém.[40] Carlo brought home a religious medal to commemorate their visit and took many photos of the church to add to the eucharistic miracles exhibition.

A Special Relic

While Carlo was learning about eucharistic miracles, a friend of the Acutis family who worked at Vatican Radio gave him a relic of Blessed Alexandrina Maria da Costa.[41] Carlo read a book about her life as part of his research for the exhibition.

Blessed Alexandrina Maria da Costa (1904–1955) was a mystic in Portugal who ate nothing but the Eucharist for the last thirteen years of her life. When Alexandrina was fourteen years old, she and two other young girls were sewing when three men forced open the door of the room where they were and entered. Alexandrina threw herself out of the window to save her purity and fell from a height of thirteen feet.[42] As a result of the fall, she eventually became completely paralyzed. For the last thirty years of her life, she was unable to leave her bed. Initially, after her injury, she constantly prayed that she would be healed. Then she eventually came to understand that she was called to endure her suffering. One day, when Alexandrina was praying, she thought: "Jesus, you are a prisoner in the tabernacle, and I am in my bed by your will. We will keep company."

This ignited a sense of mission in Alexandrina to be like the lamb of the tabernacle. The Vatican biography of her says: "In every Mass, she offered herself to the Eternal Father as a victim for sinners." She had mystical experiences of Christ's Passion every Friday from October 1938 to March 1942—182 experiences in all. Alexandrina stopped eating completely, living only on the Eucharist, from March 1942 onward. Doctors closely observed her for forty days in 1943, nearly one year after she began this fast. On October 12, 1955, she asked for the anointing of the sick, and she died the following day.*

Blessed Alexandrina was beatified by Pope John Paul II

* Note that Carlo died on October 12.

in April 2004, when Carlo was twelve. At the beatification Mass, the pope said that Blessed Alexandrina's life was "permeated and burning with this anxiety of love" in which she "wished to deny nothing to her Savior".[43] He said: "With the example of Blessed Alexandrina, expressed in the trilogy 'suffer, love, make reparation,' Christians are able to discover the stimulus and motivation to make 'noble' all that is painful and sad in life through the greatest evidence of love: sacrificing one's life for the beloved."

Carlo considered the relic of Blessed Alexandrina one of his most precious possessions.[44]

9

A Deepening Faith

Preteen years can be challenging. Not yet an adult, but no longer simply a child, Carlo had to navigate changing dynamics at school, and he gained a new responsibility at his parish. In middle school, he continued studying at the Tommaseo Institute, where he was known for being gregarious and approachable. As he left his apartment building for school each day, Carlo enthusiastically greeted the doorman, who remembers: "His eyes were filled with love, always so friendly that he seemed never to have been touched by any adversity. With his candor, he put people at ease and would listen to anyone who needed it."[1]

Middle School

Like many students in middle school, Carlo had to learn how to stand up to bullies. He befriended a classmate named Andrea who had mental disabilities. When Andrea was being teased and bullied, Carlo stood up for him. Ondina, one of Carlo's middle school classmates, remembers: "We had a mentally disabled boy in our class who was often teased and mocked by many, but Carlo was always ready to defend him."[2] A teacher observed that, as a result, sometimes Andrea could be overly clingy with Carlo. When the teacher confronted Carlo about it, he replied: "He is a great friend of mine, and I want to help him."[3]

Carlo's middle school record shows that he was not always a model student. Disciplinary notes from his school principal record times when Carlo was disruptive in class, mostly due to laughing at jokes. "Acutis acts like a clown", says one of the notes. Another: "Acutis is disruptive. Did not do homework."[4]

Throughout his school years, Carlo was never at the top of his class, but he was a curious learner, full of questions.[5] He liked to read and learn on his own, and he taught himself many things, from computer programs to playing the saxophone.[6] He loved to read the newspapers that his father passed down to him and to discuss the news with his dad. At one point, Carlo even expressed a desire to become a journalist.[7] His grandmother Luana remembers that after watching the news on TV, Carlo would pray about the news he had heard.[8]

Carlo studied English as a foreign language at his school. His English teacher remembers that Carlo had a positive attitude and was always smiling.[9] He had a talent for foreign languages and also knew and loved Spanish.[10] Carlo used his English skills to explain the Catholic Mass to Rajesh's mother, who later asked to be baptized.[11]

The Acutis family employed a tutor named Elisa, who came to their apartment three times a week to help Carlo with his homework.[12] Carlo would sometimes invite her to come with him to Mass afterward.[13] Elisa, like so many others in Carlo's life, later said that she grew in her faith because of her relationship with Carlo.[14]

Carlo had a great love of and sensitivity toward animals. One time when Carlo was playing with some other children, a boy threw a stone at a lizard and killed it. Carlo was so upset that the innocent creature had been killed, his mother recalls, that he nearly started crying.*

During Carlo's lifetime, the Acutis family owned four dogs, two cats, and some goldfish. Carlo's mother remembers vividly how she and Carlo together picked out their first dog, named Chiara. The two spotted the small black dog with a white spot on her chest in the window of a pet store in Milan and couldn't resist bringing her home.[15] The dog quickly became "an irreplaceable playmate" for Carlo.[16]

When Carlo was about ten years old, Chiara had puppies, and Carlo "became a midwife and helped with the birth".[17] The Acutis family ended up keeping two of the puppies: Stellina and the runt of the litter, Poldo. Carlo got another special dog in 2005 that looked like a Miniature Doberman. He named the dog Briciola, a common pet name in Italy that means "Breadcrumb". His cats were named Bambi and Cleo.

Carlo used his family's camcorder to create short films starring one or more of his family's many pets. He sometimes recruited Rajesh to help him record the videos, and lots of laughter ensued. Antonia remembers, "Every now and then, he would invite his friends over to see these films, complete with popcorn, Coca-Cola, and various other

* Carlo's mother believes that he was about thirteen years old when this incident with the lizard occurred. Antonia Salzano Acutis and Paolo Rodari, *Il segreto di mio figlio. Perché Carlo Acutis è considerato un santo* (Milan: Piemme, 2021), 200–1.

goodies."[18] Rajesh recalls that Carlo also liked watching *The Simpsons* and the Jurassic Park movies with his friends.[19]

Sacrament of Confirmation

Carlo's preteen years were marked by the Sacrament of Confirmation in the Catholic Church. According to the *Catechism*, baptized Christians who receive this sacrament "are more perfectly bound to the Church and are enriched with a special strength of the Holy Spirit".[20]

Before Carlo's Confirmation, his mother called the religious sisters at the convent where he received his First Communion. The sisters assured Carlo of their prayers as he prepared for the sacrament.

Carlo was confirmed just after his twelfth birthday, on May 24, 2003, at his parish church, Santa Maria Segreta. Monsignor Luigi Testore, an episcopal vicar of the Archdiocese of Milan, offered the Confirmation Mass.[21] During the Confirmation, as Monsignor Testore anointed Carlo's forehead with oil, the twelve-year-old received the "spiritual seal" of the Holy Spirit. The priest prayed for Carlo to receive the Holy Spirit as a helper and guide, granting him "the spirit of wisdom and understanding, the spirit of right judgment and courage, the spirit of knowledge and reverence".[22]

The day after Carlo's Confirmation, the Acutis family visited the cloistered community of the Romite Sisters of Saint Ambrose ad Nemus. Carlo confided in Rajesh that he felt that the Sacrament of Confirmation helped to deepen his devotion to the Eucharist. "He told me that when he received the Sacrament of Confirmation, he felt inside him [something] like a mysterious force that had enveloped him and that since then, his eucharistic devotion had increased", Rajesh said. "When I received the Sacrament of Confirmation, I felt the same thing."[23]

Defending the Faith

Confirmation empowered Carlo with the gifts of the Holy Spirit and strengthened him to spread and defend the Catholic faith. Carlo's confirmation sponsor, Sidi Perin, was passionate about training Carlo to explain the faith. Sidi liked to challenge Carlo by asking him tough questions. In Sidi's testimony to the Vatican, he recounted posing this series of questions to Carlo:

"In your opinion, is the host after the Consecration only a symbol that allows us to remember Jesus and the Last Supper?"

"In the Eucharist, Jesus is really present with his Body, his Blood, his Soul, and his Divinity, and it is not a symbol", Carlo replied.[24]

Sidi asked him again: "But when you eat the consecrated host, it has the same taste, the same smell, the same color. How can it be the Body, Blood, Soul, and Divinity of Jesus?"

Carlo did not hesitate to explain the process of transubstantiation. "The substance of the host before the Consecration is the substance of the bread, but after the Consecration, it becomes the substance of the Body, Blood, Soul, and Divinity of Jesus Christ, and the species of bread remain the same even after the Consecration, so their taste, smell, and color do not change", he said.

And then Sidi asked: "But what is the substance?"

"The deepest essence", Carlo said.

Sidi also challenged Carlo to explain papal primacy. He

recalls that Carlo immediately cited Jesus' words to Peter as recorded in the Gospel of Matthew: "You are Peter, and on this rock I will build my Church, and the gates of Hades shall not prevail against it. I will give you the keys of the kingdom of heaven, and whatever you bind on earth shall be bound in heaven, and whatever you loose on earth shall be loosed in heaven" (Mt 16:18–19).[25]

"It was clearly Jesus who established the pope as the head" was young Carlo's reply.[26]

Marian Devotion

Sidi had known Carlo since Carlo was little more than five years old.[27] He accompanied Carlo in 1997 when the boy wanted to join the Compagnia di Maria Riparatrice (Company of Mary Reparatrix). That organization was formed in Milan in 1948 to spread devotion to the Blessed Virgin Mary by promoting acts of personal consecration to Our Lady.[28] Its members, after making a consecration to Mary's Immaculate Heart, each received a Miraculous Medal blessed by a priest. Sidi was present when Carlo made his act of consecration to the Blessed Virgin Mary* in Milan's Church of Saint Anthony,[29] along with Carlo's cousins, whom Carlo had invited to join him in making the consecration.[30] Each received a miraculous medal with a blue ribbon.[31]

After making their acts of consecration, Carlo and his cousins were walking in front of Milan's great Gothic cathedral when they noticed a group of young people handing

* According to the Vatican documents, Carlo made seven acts of consecration to the Blessed Virgin Mary throughout his life, the first having been at the Shrine of Our Lady of the Rosary of Pompeii at the age of five. Carbone, *Originali o fotocopie*, 135, quoting *Positio*, 319.

out rosaries to tourists and passersby.* Carlo delighted in this unexpected gift from Our Lady and spoke to his cousins about the importance of spreading devotion to the Rosary.[32]

Catechist

With the reception of the sacrament, Carlo received the power of the Holy Spirit and was entrusted with a mission to witness to Christ "to the ends of the earth", the same mission that Jesus had charged his first disciples with before his Ascension. Not long after his Confirmation, while he was still in middle school, Carlo volunteered to help prepare other young people for the sacrament, and Monsignor Poma entrusted Carlo with a group of students who were preparing for Confirmation.[33]

Carlo took his responsibility as a catechist very seriously. When he asked his parents' permission to take on the new activity, they granted it on the condition that it would not detract from his studies. Carlo's father, Andrea, recalled: "When he became a catechist, I noticed in him a remarkable maturity, a more determined commitment."[34]

* The young people belonged to the Opera Fratel Ettore (Work of Brother Ettore), according to Carlo's mother. Servant of God Ettore Boschini was a lay brother in the Camillian Order who dedicated his life to ministering to homeless men and women in Milan.

10

Heroic Virtue Online

Carlo was thirteen years old when Pope John Paul II died on April 2, 2005. It was the vigil of Divine Mercy Sunday, a feast in the Catholic Church that the pope had himself established. Seventeen days later, white smoke rose out of the chimney atop the Sistine Chapel: cardinal electors had chosen Joseph Ratzinger to be the next pope. He took the name Benedict XVI.

The election of Benedict XVI was the first papal conclave in the Catholic Church to take place in the Internet age. To mark this historic transition, the U.S. Library of Congress compiled a digital Web archive with a collection of Catholic websites from April 2005 to November 2005;[1] the archive gives an idea of the websites that Carlo might have browsed as he researched eucharistic miracles and helped design his parish website.

By 2005, Wikipedia was already one of the most popular reference websites on the Internet. "The free encyclopedia", featuring openly editable content from online users, began in English with its first edit in 2001. Four months later, Wikipedia launched its Italian-language version. The first Wikipedia page on "Jesus"—written by the site's co-founder Jimmy Wales on March 3, 2001, at 1:12 A.M.—had been edited more than nine thousand times by the end of 2005.[2] A new era and medium of Christian discourse had begun.

At the time of the conclave, the number of broadband

Internet connections was finally beginning to surpass dial-up connections in advanced economies, which made the launch of YouTube possible in 2005, followed soon by the first-ever Internet cat video.

Most Catholic websites in the early 2000s were pretty basic in terms of graphics and format when compared with websites of multinational media companies, such as the BBC and Yahoo, at the time. Christians shared thoughts on the election of a new pope on personal online blogs.[3] Online users exchanged views on Catholic message boards. Catholic news was reported online by *America* magazine, Catholic News Service, *Inside the Vatican*, Religion News Service, and ACI Digital. And Catholic news aggregators, such as New Advent, collected links to those articles in one place. Dioceses and bishops' conferences from India to Lithuania had websites that announced the papal transition.[4]

The Internet of the early 2000s can be described as a bit quirky, and its Catholic pages were no exception. During the papal conclave, the cardinals who convened in the Sistine Chapel incommunicado were likely completely unaware that a webpage had emerged online with a bright blue background and a pasted image of the Vatican City flag beside a banner that read: "Dennis for Pope". The anonymous creator of the site (likely Dennis) promised in red text, "The papal election is here! Remember: Vote Dennis for Pope, and good things will happen."[5] Websites such as WordPress and Myspace, which were both launched in 2003, allowed users to create their own pages easily and to customize them by using basic HTML and CSS code to fill those pages with images, colorful backgrounds, special fonts, and music.

Unlike many of his young peers with an aptitude for coding in the early 2000s, Carlo did not capitalize on his technical skills in a bid to "get rich quick". He did not create an online business or a webpage with paid advertisements.

Instead, he used technology to research and connect people to the supernatural reality that we live in—one in which miracles are possible and God himself is present on Earth in the Eucharist. Carlo also used his computer skills to inform high school students of volunteering opportunities, thus facilitating charitable works.[6] The teenager's "heroic virtue" in his use of technology is an example for those who are tempted to use the Internet to feed their vices.

The Seven Deadly Sins Online

The online world provides ample temptation to give in to the seven deadly sins—pride, greed, wrath, envy, lust, gluttony, and sloth—but Carlo mastered the Internet to practice *the opposite* of each.

With its seemingly endless possibilities for entertainment and information, the Internet posed for Carlo the temptation to sloth, or acedia, by wasting hours and hours on the computer. "Acedia" comes from the Greek word *akēdia*, which means "lack of care" and can manifest itself in listlessness, distraction, and a desire to avoid the task at hand[7]—one example being fruitless scrolling online. The Internet contains a glut of information, full of rabbit holes ready to be jumped down. It takes self-restraint and temperance to sift through the distractions and find what is most important.

In the early 2000s, there were plenty of ways for people to distract themselves online, yet Carlo managed to use the computer constructively, consistent with what he once told a friend: "Every minute that passes is one less minute we have available to sanctify ourselves."[8]

Carlo most famously used his time online to focus on "the source and summit of the Christian life"[9]—the Eucharist—by researching and finding information about eucharistic miracles around the world to share with others. The official Vatican decree on Carlo Acutis' heroic virtue signed in 2018 states that he had "a rare competence in the field of information technology" and that he "chose to use his computer talent to plan and carry out an international exhibition on 'Eucharistic Miracles': an extensive photographic review of the main Eucharistic miracles that occurred over the centuries in different countries of the world".[10]

The decree also cites Carlo's contribution to a website linked to the Vatican's website (vatican.va)—that is, the webpage for the Pontifical Academy Cultorum Martyrum, where his mother had served as a curator since 2000. Pier Luigi Imbrighi, the secretary of that pontifical academy, said that Carlo "used the modern means of computer communication in which he was an extraordinary expert, helping us with great willingness and dedication in the creation of our website at vatican.va".[11] Carlo's mother wrote in her memoir that her son helped to research the lives of Catholic martyrs for the Vatican website and that he was particularly impressed by the story of Albanian Jesuit Father Anton Luli, who suffered seventeen years of imprisonment and eleven years of forced labor under Communist rule.[12]

Others have testified how Carlo helped in the creation of a website for his parish, Santa Maria Segreta. Young Carlo assisted a computer engineering student from the Polytechnic University of Milan in creating the parish website. The university student said: "From the beginning, during our discussions, I became aware of his passion for computer science, which he shared with me. His talent, outstanding for his age, surprised me on one hand and, on the other, spurred me to continue my studies."[13]

In 2005, Carlo highlighted a quote in his notes on his laptop from the Synod of Bishops on the Eucharist as the Source and Summit of the Life and Mission of the Church, presided over by Pope Benedict XVI.[14] Carlo had saved this line on his computer for further reflection:

> The Eucharist manifests that the Church and the future of the human race are bound together in Christ and in no other reality. He is the one, truly lasting rock. Therefore, Christ's victory is the Christian People who believe, celebrate, and live the Eucharistic mystery.[15]

"Carlo was fascinated by Pope Benedict", his mother said, noting that Carlo closely followed from Italy the news of Benedict XVI's visit to Cologne, Germany, for World Youth Day.[16]

A portion of the Vatican decree on Carlo's heroic virtue from the Dicastery for the Causes of Saints highlights, in particular, his use of technology: "His mastery in the use of the computer makes him an example for the use of the internet and social networks, which are not only lawful but also fruitful for good."[17] The decree adds: "His apostolic intuition to bring the light and joy of Christ through the new means of social communication makes him a pioneer in this field."

Carlo told his parents that he believed that "God creates all men with the potential to be saints; it is up to us to put into practice the unique and unrepeatable plan that God has always had in mind for each of us. We are all called to be like John, beloved disciples, united to his eucharistic Heart."[18]

"Non Io, ma Dio"

The temptation to be prideful and vain is especially acute online, particularly with social media. According to the *Oxford English Dictionary*, the earliest known use of the term "selfie" was in 2002, when Carlo was eleven years old. Although Carlo loved the computer, he did not use it to make himself loved by posting photos of himself or calling for attention. Instead, he loved to repeat the phrase "Not me, but God".[19] He liked that phrase because it rhymed in Italian: *Non io, ma Dio.*[20] Carlo expressed a similar sentiment in another quote attributed to him: "Sadness is looking at oneself; happiness is looking toward God."[21]

Blessed Are the Pure in Heart

Another unfortunate temptation that the Internet brings is lust. The success of the World Wide Web brought a "silent epidemic" of teenage pornography addiction, documented in the early 2000s.[22] A 2005 survey found that 42 percent of Internet-using youth between the ages of ten and seventeen had seen pornography.[23] Another study found that the number of teens viewing pornography online increased between 2000 and 2005.* Carlo's parents recall that their son had some difficult conversations about sin and temptation with his friends who were frequently watching porn.[24] Carlo "saw the Internet as a way to reach people, but he also would say how terrible [it was] that the Internet would be used by the devil, especially, even then, with pornography", his mother said.[25] Federico, one of Carlo's classmates from junior high school, testified the following to the Vatican:

> [For Carlo,] premarital chastity was a virtue, and it was clear to him that this entailed commitment, discipline, and a little work. But it did not seem to him that this effort was not worth the work. . . . It was obvious that he had

* The study found that intentional pornography exposure increased from 13 percent to 22 percent for boys between 2000 and 2005. Emily Rothman and Kimberly Mitchell, "A Trend Analysis of U.S. Adolescents' Intentional Pornography Exposure on the Internet, 2000–2010", Boston University School of Public Health, https://sites.bu.edu/rothmanlab/files/2019/09/porn-trends-report-version.pdf.

> values. As for chastity, I have already mentioned how important it was for him to be faithful to the teachings of the Church. . . . He was never vulgar in any of his expressions.[26]

Silvia, the mother of one of Carlo's friends whom he met often, observed that Carlo was "not afraid to express his convictions regarding purity and premarital relationships".[27] She said: "I remember the discussions he had with my son and his classmates on the afternoons when they were together. They were . . . convictions rooted in the heart." Carlo's mother recalls one instance when Carlo was at the public swimming pool and noticed that a couple was taking their public displays of affection too far. Carlo reported them to the lifeguard because it was inappropriate in the presence of children playing in the pool.[28] Junio Massimo, Carlo's cousin who was six months older than he, remembers that in one of their conversations about chastity, Carlo told him: "Being upright and just always pays off."[29] Relatedly, Carlo's parents testified to the Vatican that their son once said: "What does it profit a man to win a thousand battles if he is not then able to conquer himself with his corrupt passions?"[30] He also repeated words that echoed Saint Paul's teaching in the First Letter to the Corinthians, telling friends and family that "our bodies are temples of the Holy Spirit."[31]

11

Carlo's Confessors

Carlo met often with Father Ilio Carrai, a priest whom his mother has often referred to as Carlo's "spiritual father". Antonia had been referred to Father Ilio by a friend when Carlo was young and full of questions about the Catholic faith that she had felt ill-equipped to answer. This priest, who at the time was based in Bologna, helped to guide her back to the practice of the faith.[1] In her memoir, Carlo's mother wrote that she traveled from Milan to Bologna, a distance of about 130 miles, to see Father Ilio for spiritual direction once a month from the spring of 1995 until he died in March 2010.[2] She described the priest as "another Padre Pio".[3]

Father Ilio was known for having a deep spirituality and frequently offered spiritual direction to Carlo. At one point, the two met as often as once a month.[4] The priest said, "He came to see me every month in Bologna; almost always the young Carlo asked to confess at the end of the meetings. The severity of judgment that Carlo applied to himself led him to confess even the slightest shortcomings."[5]

Carlo confided in Father Ilio about some of his most intimate experiences with God and the supernatural, including a dream Carlo said he had had before he was five years old about his deceased grandfather being in purgatory.[6] The priest said in a written testimony, signed a few months after Carlo's death: "When he was six years old, a few months before making his First Communion, Carlo saw Jesus, who smiled at him and blessed him."[7] His spiritual director added: "Carlo was a profoundly honest child, so I thought his story was plausible, but I tried not to give it too much importance so that the child would not become too attached to these special graces that are not important for holiness."

Ilio was born in the Italian port city of Livorno before World War I, and he joined the Congregation of the Barnabite Fathers. He eventually moved and was incardinated into the Diocese of Reggio Emilia, where he taught classical literature and Latin to young people.[8]

Before Father Ilio died in 2010, he wrote that Carlo was "particularly sensitive to whether the priests were celebrating Mass in a devout manner".[9] He said that Carlo noticed and was saddened when it seemed that priests were not "fully immersed in the eucharistic celebration". Father Ilio remembered that Carlo once told him:

> Priests are the outstretched hands of Christ. They must witness to the Lord with enthusiasm, and they must be luminous models and not automated transmitters of a liturgical rite in which they do not put their hearts and through which their faith in God does not shine.[10]

Carlo also asked Father Ilio how he could better persuade people to attend Sunday Mass. The priest wrote:

> More than once, he asked me for advice on how better to persuade some people who did not attend Sunday Mass, and he told me that when he talked about the eucharistic miracle of Lanciano and the apparition of the Angel of the Eucharist to the shepherd children of Fátima, people seemed to light up.
>
> I would always encourage him to bring them the Word of the Lord when opportunities presented themselves to

> him. I was very pleased with his great apostolic zeal and had a strong hope that one day Carlo would choose a priestly path.[11]

Carlo also expressed sadness at the way some of his friends were living and asked Father Ilio for advice on how to help them to make better choices. The priest said:

> Once he was very disappointed that some of his classmates were in favor of abortion, masturbation, and premarital intercourse, and he told me that he had found it very difficult to argue with these classmates and convince them that it was not right to behave in that way. He often asked me for advice on how to help his friends to live in a way consistent with their Baptism.[12]

During his meetings with Father Ilio, Carlo would update the priest on the progress he had made and the challenges he faced in his spiritual life, such as overcoming distractions in prayer. Father Ilio said: "He told me that he had succeeded in achieving very positive results through eucharistic adoration. Carlo told me that he was finally able not to be distracted anymore during eucharistic adoration and that, thanks to that, his love for the Lord had increased a lot."[13] At the end of one of these spiritual-direction sessions, Father Ilio recalled that Carlo asked him to pray for him "so that God may make me holy".[14]

Discarding the Weights

In teaching catechism, Carlo described going to Confession and being reconciled with God as "rekindling the fire in your hot-air balloon and discarding the stones that are weighing your basket down".[15] The Vatican's records show how Carlo proposed this analogy:

> The hot air balloon, in order to ascend to the heights, needs to unload weights, just as the soul, in order to rise to heaven, needs to remove small weights, which are venial sins. If, by chance, there is a mortal sin, the soul falls back to earth, and Confession is like the fire that makes the hot air balloon rise to heaven. One must confess often because the soul is very complex.[16]

Carlo frequently went to Confession to Father Mario Parego at his parish a few blocks away from his home. His mother shared that one time when she and Carlo went to Confession, "I told Carlo to go ahead of me; then I went too, and he [the parish priest] told me that that boy was really special."[17]

Carlo also spoke to his friends about the importance of going to Confession. Mattia, his friend from Assisi, remembers: "Every now and then, he spoke to me about the importance of receiving Communion and told me to go to Confession often."[18] According to his postulator, Carlo was convinced that "if people were truly aware of the risk they run by violating God's commandments, they would be much more careful not to commit serious sins and would do more to admonish their brothers and sisters who are living inconsistently with the Baptism they have received."[19]

Umberto, Carlo's cousin, testified that Carlo once told him: "Even venial sins must be confessed because from small sins one can get to mortal ones. Our world is full of temptations, and one must confess often to be in friendship with God."[20]

Carlo also made an impression on some of the Franciscan friars in Assisi. One friar recalled, "I remember in the period when he came to Assisi, some friars said to me, 'Do you know Carlo? He spends a lot of time in eucharistic adoration.'"[21] At first, the friar did not think too much about it, but then he was amazed to learn that the boy liked to say, "People who place themselves before the sun get tanned; people who place themselves before the Eucharist become saints."[22]

12

High School Holiness

Carlo entered high school in September 2005 at the age of fourteen. His parents enrolled him in the Leo XIII Institute, a co-ed Jesuit high school. About a ten-minute walk from the Acutis family apartment in the center of Milan, the Leo XIII Institute consists of an eight-story brick building with a front courtyard filled with park benches and a fairly large campus with soccer fields, a basketball court, and a swimming pool. The high school's namesake, Pope Leo XIII, led the Church from 1878 to 1903. The school was founded during Leo's pontificate in 1893, the year in which the pope celebrated his fiftieth anniversary as a bishop.[1] At the time Carlo attended, the Jesuit high school was described as one of the "most prestigious private schools in Milan".[2]

Lending a Helping Hand to Classmates

High school curricula in Italy are often much more specialized than those in the United States. At the age of thirteen or fourteen, students pick a track—such as science, fine arts, teacher training, or classical studies—that sets a trajectory for their future studies and career paths. Carlo entered Leo XIII's classical program, which meant that he began his studies in a five-year curriculum focused on history, Latin, Greek, philosophy, biology, mathematics, and Italian literature. Carlo's classmates remember that he was always happy to help others with homework questions, especially if helping involved the computer.

Entering high school is a difficult transition for many teenagers. Insecurities and fear of rejection can cause teens to withdraw socially and emotionally. Yet Carlo did not get caught up in teenage self-absorption at the expense of those around him. He remained attentive to the needs of others. Carlo's classmates have recalled how he provided a listening ear for their worries during the first months of high school. One student said:

> I remember an episode that happened around October 2005. One day, as we were leaving school, we were taking our bicycles to go home. I confided to [Carlo] that I feared that with the arrival of the first grades for in-class assignments, the jokes and "insults" that had marked my middle and elementary school years would return.
>
> Carlo calmed me down and told me that if I needed him, he would always be there to help me. Carlo not only showed this attitude toward me, but he also remained very close to two other classmates who had shown problems in interacting with others, and he pushed them to socialize.[3]

Another classmate recalled, "When I wasn't doing well at school . . . he immediately offered to help me with math, in which he was particularly good. He also told me that he went to Mass every day, which was strange for a boy."[4]

A Boy Who "Never Concealed His Choice of Faith"

Father Roberto Gazzaniga served as the high school chaplain when Carlo was a student. He noticed right away that Carlo seemed to be more serious about his faith than most of his peers.[5] The priest said, "Carlo used to go to the chapel in the morning before entering the classroom and during breaks and would stop to pray. Nobody else did that."[6]

Gazzaniga recalls one instance in which one of the Jesuit priests at the high school gave a presentation to the freshman class about an extracurricular group called Christian Life Community. At the end of the presentation, only one student volunteered to be part of the group: Carlo, who innocently said, "I am interested in the gospel program you have described"[7]—without fear of what his classmates who snubbed the program would think.

Carlo "never concealed his choice of faith", Gazzaniga said. "Even in conversations and discussions with his classmates, he was respectful of the positions of others but without renouncing the clear vision of the principles that inspired his Christian life."[8] The Jesuit chaplain described Carlo as having had "a transparent and joyous interior life that united love for God and people in a joyful and true harmony".[9] He said: "One could point to him and say: here is a happy and authentic young man and Christian."

Many of Carlo's classmates testified as part of the process of his beatification.[10] Monsignor Ennio Apeciti, who was involved with the diocesan phase of the cause, said that Carlo's peers found him fascinating:

> All of them testified that their classmate had something special that made being with him attractive and captivating: a mixture, I would say, of candor and confidence. They joked with Carlo but never in a brash or vulgar way. He was friendly, open, and welcoming, but he also exhibited behavior with clear-cut convictions that made many of these friends mature as well.[11]

One of Carlo's classmates, who had not been baptized, said that Carlo had several conversations with him about what Baptism means and why it is so important.[12] This is similar to what another friend, who was not a practicing Catholic, shared about his time spent with Carlo:

> Sometimes when I went to his house to study or to spend some time with him, it happened that we stopped to talk about the importance of going to Mass, which he considered fundamental because I was not a practicing Catholic, and he tried to convince me of his idea. To explain his convictions to me, he sometimes used texts about eucharistic miracles.[13]

Devoted Volunteer and Faithful Friend

Having learned that Carlo was good with technology and had helped to put together a website for his parish, Father Gazzaniga reached out to him for technological help: "I asked Carlo to make a PowerPoint about the volunteer activities that the school offered for the students. Carlo was very good at utilizing tools from photography to voice editing to everything else. Carlo was very capable and knowledgeable."[14] Carlo's mother wrote in her memoir that her fifteen-year-old son devoted much of the summer of 2006 to working on both the eucharistic miracles exhibition and "the Jesuit site dedicated to volunteering", sometimes staying up until 3:00 A.M. working on those projects.[15] Unfortunately, Carlo's health took a sudden turn for the worse before he was able to participate in many of the volunteering and charitable opportunities that he had helped to promote to his classmates.[16]

Gazzaniga remembers Carlo most of all as someone who was "an excellent friend" to his classmates. "He was especially attentive to those who had the most difficulties", he said. "His charitable service was to approach and enter into friendship with people who were struggling the most."[17]

Pro-Life Witness

Carlo's classmates recall that he was not shy about sharing his pro-life views at school and that he had the courage to stand up for his convictions. One classmate said this:

> I remember this episode in particular. One day at school, there was a discussion in class about some topics, including the issue of abortion. On this occasion, Carlo showed himself to be coherent [in explaining] his principles by proclaiming himself against it and defending the right to life as a prerogative of all living beings and as a priceless and sacred value since it is granted to us by the Lord.[18]

Fabrizio, the teacher present in the classroom, said that Carlo made "a resolute, courageous speech, a strong defense of the value of life from the moment of conception in the womb". Carlo "showed particular love and determination in wanting to convince his classmates that, in the face of the wonder of unborn life, there can be no sufficiently valid reasons to interrupt its development".[19]

Carlo's stand for life made an impression in the classroom. Multiple students recalled this episode when asked about what Carlo was like in high school. One student testified: "He was strongly opposed to abortion, which he considered the murder of an innocent life."[20] Another student said: "I remember in particular a discussion about abortion in which he supported the position of the Church, defending the value of the life of the embryo, which is also a child of God."[21]

The mother of Carlo's friend Federico remembers overhearing a conversation about abortion between a group of boys who had come to her home:

> There was one boy in particular who said that the Church's positions were outdated, out of step with modern times. While the other boys kept quiet, perhaps because it was a topic that was beyond their horizon, Carlo—in a way that struck me because of his firmness and decisiveness—said clearly that it was not right because it was still murder.
>
> And he defended his position vigorously and to the last, without giving up or stopping the discussion because it was too heated. I remember saying to myself, "This guy is not shallow at all. He has very clear principles and values on which to base his life." And at that age, it didn't seem typical, but rather special. I noticed that Carlo spoke firmly, but not in a mean way.[22]

A Humble Witness

Unlike many of his peers at the private Jesuit high school, Carlo did not care about dressing in brand-name clothes to try to fit in.[23] When his mother bought him a new pair of tennis shoes, he asked her if they could return them and give the money to the poor instead. Rajesh was struck by Carlo's response when he asked the boy what the house of one of his wealthy friends was like. Carlo replied: "Like all houses, it has rooms, a kitchen, a bathroom."[24]

Carlo's parents noted that their son was not superficial at all and "was not interested in all those things that his peers boasted about, such as what kind of car his father had or how big his house was".[25]

His mother remembers: "I always had to fight with him to buy him clothes. . . . He liked to dress in a classic style and didn't like to follow fashion. He told me not to throw money away so that we could help the poor more."[26] Carlo also pushed back when his mother was about to buy sunscreen that cost about fifty euros; he was shocked by the price, asking if that was a necessary expense.[27] "Once we almost had a fight because I wanted to buy him two pairs of sneakers and he said that one was enough", she said.[28]

After Carlo's bicycle was stolen, his mother told him that she would buy him another one just like it. But Carlo insisted that he did not want another fancy bike but was content to use an old one that had been forgotten in the garage. He fixed it up and started riding it, although it was rather rickety, his mother recalls.[29]

One of Carlo's classmates described him as "humble like few others", adding "he never boasted about what he had, and if he had the chance, he would share everything with others. He always thought of others first and then of himself."[30] Carlo's parish priest, Monsignor Poma, has noted that Carlo did not try to call attention to himself, but he had "excellent qualities of responsiveness and friendliness in conversation".[31] Whereas many people are tempted to prioritize their own activities before prayer, Carlo always made time for God. "Carlo was happy when he stood before the Lord", Monsignor Poma said.[32] "Carlo was a boy who was so sweetly unaware of his extraordinary personal qualities."

Helping the Homeless

Carlo volunteered sometimes at a nearby soup kitchen run by Capuchin friars on Viale Piave in Milan.[33] Carlo's mother recalls: "With his savings, he bought sleeping bags for homeless people, and in the evening, he brought them some hot drinks."[34] The postulator of Carlo's cause has said:

> From childhood, he showed great charity toward others. His love was extraordinary, first of all for his parents and then for the poor, the homeless, the marginalized, and the elderly who were abandoned and alone. He used the savings from his weekly pocket money to help beggars and those who slept outdoors. He organized fairs in the parish to help the missions with the funds raised.[35]

Carlo befriended a missionary religious sister, Sister Giovanna Negrotto, who said that Carlo took a particular interest in her missionary work in India, always asking to know more about her "great leper friends".[36]

Carlo's grandmother Luana remembers that Carlo did not want her to spend money on him and that he was very sensitive to the needs of the poor where they lived, in both Milan and Assisi. She said: "In Assisi, some homeless people were sleeping on the ground on the road leading to Via Santo Stefano. He let me or his mother accompany him . . . and left a sandwich and a five-euro bill next to them, which were taken from his allowance."[37]

Carlo's mother said: "In the evenings, he left the house with containers full of food and hot drinks. He would take them to the homeless near Arco della Pace, and he also bought them sleeping bags with money he had saved. He was accompanied by our servant Rajesh."[38] Carlo's friend Vanessa also recalled: "When we went out together for a walk, he had his allowance with him. If he saw some poor person, he would give it to him without keeping anything for himself."[39] An encounter with one man in particular stood out in Rajesh's memory:

> There was a man called Matteo. He was sleeping on the ground on cardboard and was cold. Carlo started to worry. He wouldn't sleep, and he thought about what he could do for the man. . . . Then he returned home and forced his Mum. "Mum, why don't you give him a sleeping bag, so he can sleep well." And he had cooking done for him too.
>
> Every evening I accompanied Carlo. He didn't bring him leftovers from our home but fresh, just-cooked food—just like we were eating. . . . He said, "This man in difficulty should eat, as we do, too." And that's what his life was like.[40]

The Premiere of the Eucharistic Miracles Exhibition

The exhibition on eucharistic miracles premiered in 2005, when Carlo was in his first year of high school. It was providential timing, as Pope John Paul II had just proclaimed the Catholic Church's Year of the Eucharist.

The exhibition, attributed to the San Clemente Institute, featured panels with photos and text—one large posterboard display for each location where a miracle occurred.[41] Its panels were displayed for two weeks in Rome in May 2005 at the Pontifical Athenaeum Regina Apostolorum, a university directed by the Legionaries of Christ.[42] The eucharistic miracles exhibition was also displayed at the International Ecclesiastical College of Saint Charles Borromeo in Rome in October and November 2005.[43]

Father Giorgio Maria Carbone saw Carlo present the posterboard panels of the eucharistic miracles exhibition in person, just outside Milan on May 27, 2006.[44] Carlo had just turned fifteen. On this day, the Acutis family's exhibition was among the displays at a conference hosted by the Italian Catholic monthly magazine *Il Timone* and the Fides

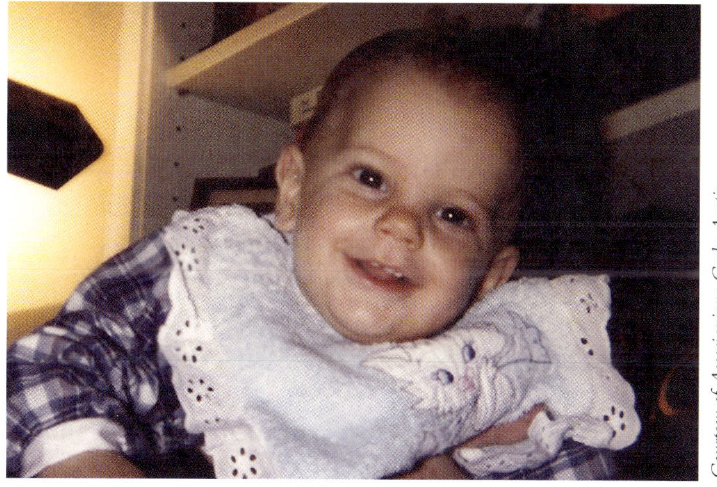

Courtesy of Associazione Carlo Acutis

Carlo as a baby. He was named after his paternal grandfather and godfather, Carlo Acutis.

Courtesy of Associazione Carlo Acutis

Carlo at six years old. At this age, he would collect spring flowers to give to the Blessed Virgin Mary.

Courtesy of Associazione Carlo Acutis

Carlo plays in front of the Basilica of Saint Anthony of Padua.

Courtesy of Associazione Carlo Acutis

Carlo on the day of his First Communion on June 16, 1998.

Courtesy of Associazione Carlo Acutis

Carlo's favorite cartoons were Transformers, Pokémon, The Smurfs, and Spiderman.

Courtesy of Associazione Carlo Acutis

Carlo with one of his beloved dogs in the Apennine Mountains in the Italian region of Umbria.

Courtesy of Associazione Carlo Acutis

Young Carlo celebrating Christmas with one of his four dogs.

Courtesy of Associazione Carlo Acutis

"My son was always sociable, lively, playful," Carlo's mother said.

Courtesy of Associazione Carlo Acutis

Carlo with Rajesh Mohur on the day of his Confirmation.

Courtesy of Associazione Carlo Acutis

Carlo learned how to ski when he visited Switzerland with his grandparents, placing second in a ski race.

Courtesy of Associazione Carlo Acutis

Carlo received his first computer as a gift in 2000 and taught himself how to code.

Courtesy of Associazione Carlo Acutis

Carlo tried many sports, including karate, tennis, volleyball, swimming, and soccer.

Courtesy of Associazione Carlo Acutis

Carlo's mother said that he was not very skilled at soccer, but he loved being with his friends.(Carlo, top row, second from the left.)

Courtesy of Associazione Carlo Acutis

Carlo on Mount Subasio. He liked to hike in the hills surrounding Assisi.

Courtesy of Associazione Carlo Acutis

Carlo during a visit to his paternal grandparents in Santa Margherita Ligure, near Portofino.

Courtesy of Associazione Carlo Acutis

Carlo celebrates a birthday in a family photo. Carlo's birthday is on May 3.

Courtesy of Associazione Carlo Acutis

Carlo in the nature preserve of the Pian Grande di Castelluccio di Norcia.

et Ratio Foundation. Cardinal Joseph Zen, who at the time was the bishop of Hong Kong, was a featured speaker at the conference. Father Carbone was at the conference to promote Catholic books published by Edizioni Studio Domenicano, a Dominican publishing house in Italy. He recalls:

> A few dozen meters away from our stand, Carlo and his parents had installed an exhibition illustrating eucharistic miracles and spoke with hundreds of visitors to explain to them the numerous miracles for which there is reliable documentation. . . . A few days earlier I had received a phone call from Antonia, Carlo's mother. We had arranged to meet at the *Il Timone* event. I knew, therefore, that I would meet Antonia. I didn't know I would also meet her husband, Andrea, and her son, Carlo.[45]

Carbone said he was surprised to learn that Carlo had helped to create the eucharistic miracles exhibition. He finally introduced himself to Carlo at the end of the long day of speaking to people who approached their tables. He remembers the encounter vividly:

> Carlo had a smile that was brimming with satisfaction and joy. He was putting the photo panels back in their boxes, like something very precious. His eyes were sparkling, almost emotional. He told me and my confreres about what he did during the day and, above all, about his joy at having been able to speak of the active and Real Presence of Jesus in the Eucharist.[46]

An Original

Carlo's mother remembers that her son used to like to say, "We are all born as originals, but many die as photocopies."[47] It is unclear where Carlo might have first heard this phrase—coined by the English poet Edward Young in the eighteenth century as: "Born Originals, how comes it to pass that we die Copies?"[48] Regardless, high school is a time when young people can face many pressures to try to "fit in"—that is, they are tempted to become the "carbon copy" of their idea of the cool kids. Carlo's fondness for this statement reflects his fearlessness of standing out. Father Carbone interprets the catchphrase in the following way: "'Dying as photocopies' is the outcome of an existence lived chasing fashions."[49] It echoes an idea by C. S. Lewis, who wrote: "How monotonously alike all the great tyrants and conquerors have been: how gloriously different are the saints."[50] Carlo's mother has said:

> Carlo understood very well, and we had spoken about it many times, that people always run the risk of going astray, of straying from the path traced out by Jesus for each one of us. He had before his eyes many examples of how one can easily go astray and spend days far from the Lord. He firmly believed that in order not to die as photocopies it was important to have recourse to the sacraments.[51]

Carlo saw "being original" not only as being true to God's plan but as a characteristic of Jesus himself. "Jesus is very original, because he hides in a piece of bread, and only God could do something so incredible", he told his parents.[52]

Carlo was not involved in many extracurricular activities during his school years, but he liked computer programming, photography, and watching movies.[53] His friend Federico remembers that Carlo liked reading a magazine about cars, but "he read the Bible with even greater interest".[54]

Carlo's friend Vanessa recalled that some of the girls in school had crushes on Carlo "because he was a good-looking guy".[55] She added: "And he did not shy away or withdraw. . . . He exuded such a sense of composure in his interactions with all girls and boys without distinction. He told me that the true love he felt was for Jesus. I remember it well: 'My true love is for Jesus.'" Vanessa also remembers that Carlo "was very respectful toward girls" and that he "never made the slightest vulgar expression".

Valentina, Carlo's former elementary school teacher who continued to run into him in the neighborhood as he was older, said that she would sometimes tease Carlo by asking him "to introduce me to his 'girlfriend'". Carlo replied that he was still too young to have a girlfriend. She said: "I liked to ask him this question because while some of his classmates introduced me to their 'girlfriends,' Carlo always showed such kind respect for girls and contentment to wait to be the 'right age' . . . spoken with that blush that revealed his modesty and purity of heart."[56]

Alessandra, one of Carlo's high school friends, recalled that "Carlo had very clear ideas about having a girlfriend. . . . It was a very important thing for him that girls were respected."[57] She said: "In fact, he scolded his friends who easily gave themselves to boys. He was a boy of great moral values and sound principles." Another one of Carlo's classmates recalled: "We used to talk all the time, and one day I remember that we talked about the importance of the Sacrament of Marriage, and I was very struck by his statement that young people must follow the teachings of the Church, which says to wait until marriage to have intimate relations."[58]

Carlo's mother once overheard him counseling his high

school friends, some of whom were already engaging in premarital sex, about relationships and the importance of respecting human dignity. She said:

> In particular, I remember . . . during the summer of 2006, the week in which we were guests of his [paternal] grandparents at the seaside. After dinner, we sat on the terrace to get some air, and he received a phone call from a friend who was a girl. He got up and moved away so as not to disturb [us], but even without meaning to, you could hear their whole conversation.
>
> I was struck by the way Carlo spoke as a "wise man" and scolded his friend, who had met a boy in a nightclub and immediately had an intimate relationship with him.* He spent an hour explaining to her the dignity of the human person and the importance of chastity. As it was getting late . . . I finally told him to cut the conversation short. And then I told him jokingly that not even the girl's father had ever given her such a lecture.[59]

Some students at Carlo's high school frequently went out drinking at clubs and used drugs. Carlo's mother remembers that her son had asked a cloistered religious order to join him in praying for these classmates.[60] She noted: "To be honest, at times it almost sounded like a priest talking, and I would smile as I listened to him tell others about the importance of the body as a 'temple of the Holy Spirit'."[61]

Summer near Portofino

The family spent part of the summer of 2006 at a house owned by Carlo's paternal grandparents near Portofino in

* In Italy, teenagers aged sixteen and over are allowed inside nightclubs and bars.

the beach town of Santa Margherita Ligure. One day, while Carlo and his family were out in his grandfather's boat, not far from the cliffs of the Cinque Terre, a school of dolphins began to jump out of the water alongside the boat. "I remember Carlo's face. He was ecstatic, radiant", his mother said.[62] She later found out that Carlo had asked Jesus in prayer to be able to see dolphins during their family vacation, as they were among his favorite animals. Antonia now sees that moment as a special grace.[63]

When the family went to dinner at a nice restaurant in Portofino one night, Carlo's mother observed that her son seemed deep in thought, that his face looked a little glum, and that he was much quieter than usual.[64] He confided in her later that night that when he was surrounded by all the wealth and opulence in Portofino, his thoughts kept coming back to Jesus' words on the Cross: "I thirst" (Jn 19:28). He had been distracted thinking of "Jesus' salvation" for the people in that restaurant.[65] Antonia said: "I was very touched by his words. . . . I understood more deeply that it is not wealth that gives happiness and that the only real concern should be the salvation of our souls and [the souls] of the people we meet."[66]

Vocational Discernment

Because of Carlo's passionate faith, many of his friends, family, and acquaintances had speculated that he might have a vocation to the priesthood. In fact, Vatican documents attest that Carlo once called the Blessed Virgin Mary "the only woman in my life".[67]

During the vacation near Portofino in the summer before his second year of high school, Carlo raised the question of his vocation with his mother. Antonia remembers that, after attending Mass, the two of them were walking along a beautiful path that runs along the sea. Carlo turned to her and asked if she thought that he should become a priest.[68] He was fifteen years old. "I didn't say much to him. I tried to make him understand that I was more interested in his happiness than anything else. If this desire to embrace religious life was something serious and heartfelt, I would have been very happy for him", she said.[69]

Carlo's mother still sometimes wonders what her son would have been like as a priest.[70] She speculates that he likely would have chosen to become a diocesan priest because he held them in such high esteem. Antonia later learned that her son had been thinking about the possibility of entering religious life for some time before approaching her to ask about the subject.[71]

A Saint for the Year

When he was in high school, Carlo enjoyed learning about the lives of different saints.* Saint Francis and Saint John the Evangelist were among his favorites, as were some of the Blesseds (such as Blessed Alexandrina Maria da Costa) whom he had learned about through working on the eucharistic miracles exhibition.

On January 1, 2006, Carlo received a holy card of Saint Alexander Sauli, who he decided would be his "patron saint for the year".[72] Alexander Sauli was a sixteenth-century

* While studying at the Jesuit high school, Carlo also learned about the life of Saint Ignatius of Loyola and had the chance to visit Manresa, Spain, where Ignatius wrote his Spiritual Exercises. Antonia Salzano Acutis and Paolo Rodari, *Il segreto di mio figlio. Perché Carlo Acutis è considerato un santo* (Milan: Piemme, 2021), 174.

priest from Milan who was Saint Charles Borromeo's confessor. Sauli was also known in his time as the "Apostle of Corsica". He was made a bishop and sent by Pope Pius V to Corsica, an island fifty miles off the coast of Italy, where the zealous priest reformed the clergy, established seminaries, and preached the gospel, thus helping the faith to flourish. In Milan, Sauli's relics can be found in the Church of Saints Paul and Barnabas.[73] His feast day is October 11, a date that the Acutis family would soon never forget.

13

"I Offer My Suffering"

Carlo's second year of high school had just started in the fall of 2006 when his mother noticed a small red spot in the corner of his right eye. He developed a fever, and his parents decided that he should stay home from school. Carlo's mother telephoned a pediatrician. The physician observed during the home visit that Carlo had inflammation in his throat, but he told his mother not to worry.[1]

On his first day home sick from school at the beginning of October, Carlo prayed a Rosary and spent time on his laptop working on his homework. Within a few days, however, he was feeling worse. He moved to the small guest bedroom across the hall from his room where he could watch television while resting in bed. Rajesh could tell Carlo was experiencing "terrible suffering" during that time at home in bed.[2] He stood in the doorway of the guest room and heard Carlo tell his mother on October 4: "All that I am suffering I offer to the Lord."[3]

The Vatican Dicastery for the Causes of Saints records Carlo's words as follows: "I offer all the suffering I will have to endure to the Lord for the pope and for the Church, in order not to go through purgatory and to go straight to heaven."[4]

Carlo believed in redemptive suffering—that is, that suffering and personal sacrifices have meaning [or value] when they are united to Christ's Passion on the Cross to accomplish God's will. According to the *Catechism*, Jesus gave new meaning to suffering through his Passion and death on the Cross: "It can henceforth configure us to him and unite us with his redemptive Passion."[5]

Carlo celebrated the feast of Saint Francis of Assisi, on October 4, in bed. His mother bought him a box of chocolates for the feast and slept on a mattress on the floor next to his bed.[6] The next day, Carlo woke up with very swollen glands, so his mother called the doctor again. He determined that Carlo likely had something like the mumps.[7] When blood appeared in Carlo's urine the following day, his mother telephoned Dr. Vittorio Carnelli.[8] The doctor referred Carlo and his family to the De Marchi Clinic to undergo some tests.

By Saturday, October 7, Carlo did not have the strength to get out of bed on his own. His parents used a rolling desk chair to wheel him from the bedroom to the elevator in their apartment building to take him to the De Marchi Clinic.[9]

While waiting for the test results at the clinic, Carlo's mother noticed that the church across the street held the relics of Saint Alexander Sauli, Carlo's chosen patron saint for that year.[10] Antonia went to Mass at the church, where she realized that the saint's feast day would be celebrated later that week, on Wednesday, October 11. In prayer, she entrusted her son to the sixteenth-century saint from Milan. In their joint testimony submitted to the Vatican, Carlo's parents recall that their son once said: "Often we live too frantically and do everything possible to forget that sooner or later we, too, will climb Golgotha. In fact, from birth, our earthly destiny is sealed because we are all invited to climb up Golgotha and take up our cross."[11]

When the test results came in, the diagnosis for fifteen-year-old Carlo was severe: acute promyelocytic leukemia (APL), a blood cancer that can lead to excessive bleeding and blood-clot formation.* After the doctor left the room, Carlo remained calm and told his mother with a smile: "The Lord gave me a wake-up call."[12] His mother said: "I was very struck by his attitude, his . . . positivity and serenity."[13]

His father called the cloistered nuns at the convent where Carlo had received his First Communion to inform them that Carlo was gravely ill.[14] The mother superior said that upon receiving that call, a line from the book of Wisdom came to her mind: "Being perfected in a short time, he fulfilled long years; for his soul was pleasing to the Lord, therefore he took him quickly from the midst of wickedness" (4:13–14).[15]

Rajesh and his niece Vanessa desperately wanted to visit Carlo in the hospital, but visitors were limited due to his serious condition. Together they called Antonia to get updates on how he was doing. Antonia passed along Carlo's words of reassurance that he was heading toward peace and happiness that cannot be found in this life.[16]

Dr. Andrea Biondi and Dr. Mòmcilo Jankovic, who treated Carlo in the pediatric clinic of Saint Gerald Hospital, wrote a short reflection together on their interactions with him in the hospital. They said:

> [Carlo] was like a meteor with a quick passage through our ward; leukemia took him away before we could get to

* Carlo had the M3 subtype of acute myeloid leukemia that affects the white blood cells known as promyelocytes. "Treatment of Children with Acute Promyelocytic Leukemia (APL)", American Cancer Society, February 12, 2019, https://www.cancer.org/cancer/leukemia-in-children/treating/children-with-apl.html.

> know him even a little. However, his sweet eyes remain ingrained [in our memories]. His gaze was full of attention . . . of courage, of love, of strong empathy. Shining through him was a faith in God that he had desired and still wanted to pass on to others, to his neighbors. . . . His gentle eyes . . . taught us a lot: life, whether short or long, should be lived intensely for oneself, but also and above all for others.[17]

One nurse wondered why Carlo did not complain of pain, given that his arms and legs were so swollen.[18]

Reflecting back on those days in the hospital, Carlo's father said that his son "seemed like a lamb that did not make a sound: not a whimper, not a whine, just kindness to everyone, from the medical and nursing staff to all of us. Yet with the knowledge that he was dying."[19] He said: "What struck me was Carlo's serenity: not a complaint, even though he was intubated and full of needles."[20]

Father Sandro Villa, the hospital chaplain of Saint Gerald Hospital, was called to give Carlo the Anointing of the Sick and Holy Communion on Tuesday, October 10, 2006. Villa said:

> In a small room, at the end of the corridor, I found myself in front of a boy. His pale but serene face surprised me —unthinkable in a seriously ill person, especially an adolescent. I was also amazed by the composure and devotion with which, albeit with difficulty, he received the two sacraments. He seemed to have been waiting for them and felt the need for them.[21]

For Villa, this administration of the sacraments would be his only encounter with Carlo, but he said that the look of serenity on Carlo's face was something that stayed with him. He said: "After a few years . . . I learned that he was declared 'Venerable.' I was amazed that the Lord had allowed me to meet him, if only for a few moments."

On October 11, 2006, Carlo slipped into a coma due to a brain hemorrhage caused by the leukemia.* It is not known what his last words were. His heart stopped beating on October 12—a date that is now celebrated as a local feast in the Diocese of Assisi and the Archdiocese of Milan. His parents had desired to donate Carlo's organs, but they were too compromised by cancer.

Carlo's Constant Offering

Death came suddenly for Carlo, but the young boy was well prepared for it by the way he had lived his life. Through Carlo's daily time spent with Christ in the Eucharist, the Lord had shown him the great beauty of offering his life as a gift of love. Showing a profound maturity beyond his years, Carlo understood that death was not a moment to be dreaded. He had learned from Jesus how to make death an act of supreme self-giving love. As Cardinal Justin Rigali wrote as he retired as archbishop of Philadelphia: "Death is the moment to give all, to surrender all with Jesus and in union with His sacrifice."[22]

Antonia has said that, up until Carlo's last day, she had been praying for a miracle to save her son, even asking for the intercession of Venerable Antonio Pietro Cortinovis, the Capuchin founder of the Work of Saint Francis for the Poor of Milan. "But God's plans were different", she said.[23]

*A cause of early death in newly diagnosed cases of acute promyelocytic leukemia is severe intracranial bleeding, or a brain hemorrhage. Severe bleeding accounts for early death in only 5 to 10 percent of patients diagnosed with APL in developed countries. Massimo Breccia et al., "Early Hemorrhagic Death Before Starting Therapy in Acute Promyelocytic Leukemia: Association with High WBC Count, Late Diagnosis and Delayed Treatment Initiation", *Haematologica* 95, no. 5 (May 2010): 853–54, https://doi.org/10.3324/haematol.2009.017962.

Carlo's father underlined that his son's undivided faith in the Lord was constant until his last breath. He said:

> Often people do not fall in love with Jesus through us Christians because we are often divided. We do not trust that our ultimate happiness can be following Jesus without reservation. Many Christians live as if God wants to take something away from them. Most of us fail to understand the wonder of God's proposal for us. Carlo understood it.
>
> He understood that he was headed toward a wonderful goal, far greater than anything we could experience in earthly life. And this made him happy. He had believed in it all the way. Until his last breath. He wanted with all his heart to go to heaven even while he was on this earth. This is perhaps his secret: not to be divided but to be in love with the Supreme Good. Carlo attracted people (including us parents) because he was really in love with God and his life was full of joy. He was truly a "little Christ".[24]

Funeral: "No Flowers, but Prayers"

Carlo's family was granted permission to bring his body from the funeral home to their apartment, where family, friends, parishioners, and classmates came to say their last goodbyes.[25]

Carlo's funeral was held on Saturday, October 14, 2006, in his parish church of Santa Maria Segreta. When Antonia arrived at the church, she found that it was already packed. She saw people she had never met before, including homeless people and strangers whom Carlo had helped over the course of his life—"a great network of friendship . . . that manifested itself at that moment in all its greatness and beauty".[26]

Carlo was remembered at his funeral as "a pleasantly approachable person" and as "a boy who loved life, very simply, and knew how to show it, almost contagiously".[27] The

Archdiocese of Milan published an excerpt of some of the words spoken at Carlo's funeral:

> Proclaiming the Good News as we celebrate the funeral of a fifteen-year-old teenager. To die at the age of fifteen, we are tempted to say: "He has not yet had his due in life." Carlo, in fact, left us at an age in which one looks to the future with optimism, with a head full of dreams and already some projects . . . with the taste of living intensely in the present.[28]

Carlo's mother is convinced that her son was interceding from heaven within days of his death. She said: "My son performed the first miracles on the day of the funeral."[29] Antonia explained that one forty-four-year-old woman from Rome who came to Milan for the funeral to say goodbye to Carlo asked him in prayer for the grace to have children. A few days after the funeral, she found out that she was pregnant.[30] Antonia also claims that another woman who had breast cancer but had not started chemotherapy asked for Carlo's intercession and was healed.[31]

The Italian newspapers *Corriere della Sera* and *La Stampa* both announced Carlo's death in a brief paragraph that requested at the end, "No flowers, but prayers".[32] An entire newspaper page was filled with condolence messages to Carlo's parents from the business associates of Carlo's father and family acquaintances in Milan, Paris, and London. Not long after Carlo's death, a priest in Milan approached Antonia to say how impressed he was by Carlo's discretion and humility, noting that he had only discovered that Carlo belonged to "an important family" through reading the newspaper obituary.[33]

Carlo's high school chaplain, Father Gazzaniga, remembers that the entire high school was shocked by the suddenness of Carlo's death. He recalls seeing Carlo for the last time in the halls of the school and telling him something like "See you on Monday." But he never saw him again.[34] "In virtually one week, Carlo was hospitalized and died", he said. Though Carlo's death was a shock to the school, some of his classmates have described how they grew closer to God after his death. One high school classmate testified: "Carlo went to Mass several times a week, he had a lot of faith, he believed in a personal conversation with the Lord, and he said the Rosary every day. After Carlo's death, I got closer to the Church, and I think it could be due to Carlo's intercession."[35]

Tixtla, Mexico: A New Eucharistic Miracle?

Nine days after Carlo died, an extraordinary event was reported in a small town in southern Mexico. A religious sister who had been helping to distribute Holy Communion during a Mass for a religious retreat in the parish of Saint Martin of Tours in the Mexican town of Tixtla approached the priest with tears in her eyes. The sister showed the priest, Father Raymundo Reyna Esteban, a host that had begun to give off a reddish substance. It begged the question: Could it be a eucharistic miracle? The priest quickly informed the bishop of Chilpancingo-Chilapa, who called for an investigation.

Though the reported miracle in Tixtla has not yet been approved by the local bishop,[36] Carlo's mother sees a clear connection with the death of her son. She added Tixtla as a panel to the eucharistic miracles exhibition and wrote in her memoir: "Before Carlo's death, I always told him to ask Jesus to perform other eucharistic miracles, similar to the one in Lanciano, where it was evident that in the consecrated host there really is His Real Presence. I think that the intercession of my son was granted . . . in Tixtla, Mexico."[37]

A Premonition?

As Carlo's parents were going through his belongings, his mother found a file on his computer that stopped her in her tracks. It was a video that Carlo had recorded of himself in July 2006, four months before his death. In the video, Carlo waved and smiled and said: "I weigh 70 kilos [154 pounds], and I'm destined to die."[38]

Father Carbone has speculated that perhaps Carlo was referring to "the transience of earthly existence" and "the vanity of the human body, which, no matter how much it grew, . . . was nevertheless destined for death".[39] But his parents believe that Carlo may have had a premonition that he had only months to live. In their joint testimony to the Vatican for his cause for sainthood, his parents wrote: "Since he was a child, he had said that he would die of a ruptured vein, which, in fact, happened because his cause of death was a cerebral hemorrhage."[40] Carlo's grandmother also remembers that her young grandson once told her: "You know, I will not live long."[41]

Carlo's Cult Grows

One year after Carlo died, Nicola Gori, a journalist at the Vatican's official newspaper, *L'Osservatore Romano*, published a book in Italian about Carlo's life titled *Eucaristia: La Mia Autostrada per il Cielo* (The Eucharist: my highway to heaven). The publication of this book made a splash in

Italy and sparked many articles sharing Carlo's story in Italian and English. News articles described Carlo as "a teen of our times" who loved computers, attended Mass daily, and offered his life for the pope and the Church. A priest in the northern Italian diocese of Vercelli published an article titled "Carlo: An Example for Many Young People."[42]

Francesca Consolini, the postulator of the causes of the saints for the Archdiocese of Milan, told journalists in 2007—one year after Carlo's death—that she believed that there was reason to open Carlo's cause of beatification after the Vatican's required five-year waiting period. She said: "His faith, which was unique in such a young person, was pure and certain. It made him always be sincere with himself and with others. He showed extraordinary care for others; he was sensitive to the problems and situations of his friends and those who lived close to him and were with him day to day."[43] Consolini added: "I should stress that he was a normal boy who was joyful, serene, sincere, and helpful and loved having company; he liked having friends."

Carlo's story began to spread quickly, thanks in part to the technology that he had particularly loved, the Internet. Within one year of Carlo's death, the Friends of Carlo Acutis Association[44] had a website dedicated to sharing his story at CarloAcutis.com.[45] The website included a page in March 2008 asking "anyone who receives graces or favors attributed to the intercession of Carlo Acutis or whoever wishes to receive free material to learn about Carlo" to write to Antonia Acutis or directly to the Office for the Causes of Saints of the Archdiocese of Milan.[46] The website also provided information for anyone who desired to visit Carlo's tomb in the Upper Assisi Cemetery.* By 2009, the association had

* Carlo's body was originally buried in a family plot in Ternengo, northeast of Turin, but in January 2007, it was transferred to the Upper Assisi Cemetery. During Carlo's last meeting with his spiritual director, Father Ilio

an official Facebook group to bring together all of Carlo's new fans,[47] and several testimonies had been uploaded to the website, including letters from two Italian priests who had been inspired by reading about Carlo's story after he died.[48]

Amid the grief of losing her only child, Antonia devoted herself to continuing to spread the eucharistic miracles exhibition to different parts of the world, sending the panels to more than five hundred parishes by 2008.[49] On November 29, 2007, she registered the domain name miracolieucaristici.org for a website about eucharistic miracles coded in HTML and CSS.[50] The website had blue hyperlinks listed beneath each country's name. Clicking on a hyperlink brought up a pdf image of the respective panel from the eucharistic miracles exhibition, displaying information and photos about each miracle allowing the viewers to "virtually visit the places where the miracles happened".[51]

As Carlo's story began to spread, people from around the world reached out to the Acutis family via the contact information listed on CarloAcutis.com. One tech-savvy priest was particularly enthusiastic: Father Marcelo Tenorio, a priest in Campo Grande, Brazil, wrote on his blog on November 4, 2012, that he felt called to an "urgent and effective mission" to spread Carlo Acutis' story "so that many young people might find God through the example of Carlo's life and that they may return to new life and be saved".[52] Tenorio's intuition and efforts led to miraculous results.

Carrai, the priest said that the fifteen-year-old had told him: "Assisi is the place where I feel the happiest." Giorgio Maria Carbone, *Originali o Fotocopie?* (Bologna: Edizioni Studio Domenicano, 2021), 188.

14

A Miracle in Brazil

Carlo died on October 12, the feast of Our Lady of Aparecida, the patron saint of Brazil. This Marian feast, celebrated each year for nearly three hundred years, has its origins in an event that three fishermen witnessed in 1717.

Domingos Garcia, Felipe Pedroso, and João Alves had set out in a boat on the Paraíba do Sul River in hope of collecting enough fish for a banquet to be held in their village. According to the local tradition, though they cast their nets for hours, the fishermen had caught nothing when João pulled out something that looked like a piece of wood. He cast his net again and found another piece of wood that fit together with the first piece to make a statue. João threw his net out for a third time, and it became filled with so many fish that he needed help to pull it into the boat.[1] Felipe placed the statue in his hut and called it Nossa Senhora da Conceição Aparecida (Our Lady of the Conception Who Appeared). News of the miraculous catch spread, and more and more people came to pray before the statue—so many that a chapel was built to house the image of Mary in 1737, and larger churches were successively built on the site in the centuries that followed.

About twelve million pilgrims visit the National Sanctuary of Aparecida in Brazil each year. Pope Francis visited the shrine of Our Lady of Aparecida while in Brazil for the 2013 World Youth Day; the international youth gathering of more than one million people was itself a confluence point where Carlo's story was spread.[2]

Less than three months after World Youth Day in Rio de Janeiro, another miracle occurred in Brazil on October 12, the same day as the miracle of the fish 296 years before. This miracle involved a three-year-old boy named Matheus Vianna. Since his birth in 2010, Matheus had suffered from significant digestive disorders.[3] His mother, Luciana Lins Vianna, took her young son in for tests, and he was diagnosed in 2012 with a rare congenital malformation of his pancreas.[4]

Matheus could hardly eat without vomiting and was therefore malnourished. He was hospitalized several times for severe dehydration. The doctors said that the only possible solution was a transplant, but it was unclear whether Matheus would be strong enough to survive such a procedure. "He used to vomit almost constantly, two minutes after eating anything. We had to give him special formula so that he could retain at least some nutrients", his mother told a Brazilian journalist.[5] "I looked for the best specialist for him to have the surgery, but she denied it. She said it was impossible because he was underweight and . . . that if he went through the surgery, he would die; he wouldn't be able to bear it."[6]

Luciana prayed constantly for her son. On October 12, she brought little Matheus with her to Mass at the parish of São Sebastião in Campo Grande, the capital city of the Mato Grosso do Sul state in central Brazil. Father Marcelo Tenorio was offering the Mass that day and brought out a relic of Servant of God Carlo Acutis.*

* At the time, Carlo was a Servant of God. Carlo was declared Venerable by the Catholic Church on July 5, 2018.

The Brazilian priest had obtained the relic—a piece of fabric from Carlo's clothes—directly from the Acutis family. Father Tenorio first learned about Carlo in 2010. He contacted the Italian association promoting his cause and was put in touch with Carlo's mother. "She gave me a book about Carlo and gave me permission to talk about him in Brazil", Tenorio said.[7] The priest shared Carlo's story with other Brazilian parishes and youth groups. He eventually traveled to Assisi, where he met with Carlo's mother, who gave him the relic.

Tenorio exposed the relic for veneration each year on the anniversary of Carlo's death and Brazil's national feast, October 12. Matheus' mother recalled:

> That day, Matheus saw the line of people standing to venerate Carlo's relic and asked me what they were doing. I told him we could pray to Carlo for anything if we wanted to because he was in heaven. Matheus was on his grandfather's lap when we approached the relic and, before my dad could touch the relic, Matheus kissed it and said out loud, "Stop vomiting!" Many people witnessed this moment.[8]

Luciana also prayed for Carlo's intercession to heal her son, and other parishioners and family members joined her.

Matheus was healed immediately after kissing the relic.[9] His mother noted that her son was particularly joyful after that Mass. When the family arrived home, Matheus ate rice, steak, beans, and French fries.[10] Luciana said: "It was the first time in his entire life that this happened [i.e., that he could eat solid foods without problems]. He had been vomiting after eating since he was born; he even rejected breast milk. Since that day, I knew he was cured because of Carlo. The change was too drastic and too sudden."[11]

Matheus began to gain weight, and doctors found that his pancreas, which had been an anatomical anomaly before, was now completely normal without surgery. "One doctor said that [Matheus] then had a textbook pancreas, an organ that is so perfect that it looks unreal", Luciana said.[12] Another doctor remarked with surprise that "Matheus's surgery had left no scars", not realizing that the needed surgery had never taken place.[13] Father Tenorio reported to the postulator of Carlo's cause for sainthood all that had happened.

Carlo's Cause for Sainthood

For Carlo, who had been a fan and friend of many saints during his short life, it was not long after his death that he was in the process to be canonized himself. The word "saint" derives from the Latin *sanctus* and means someone holy. When the pope canonizes a person, it is an official declaration by the Catholic Church that the person is in heaven.[14] The Constitution on the Sacred Liturgy *Sacrosanctum Concilium* states: "All the activities of the Church are directed, as toward their end, to the sanctification of men in Christ and the glorification of God."[15]

The Church proposes the saints as both models and intercessors. The *Catechism of the Catholic Church*, quoting John Paul II, states: "The saints have always been the source and origin of renewal in the most difficult moments in the Church's history. Indeed, 'holiness is the hidden source and infallible measure of her apostolic activity and missionary zeal.'"[16]

The process of canonization involves several steps. As a candidate for sainthood moves through the process, he receives a corresponding title for each step: Servant of God, Venerable, Blessed, and Saint. The Catholic Church requires a five-year waiting period after someone's death before a cause for sainthood can be opened in order to judge whether the person has a true and widespread "reputation for holiness" and intercessory prayer.[17]

In the five years that passed after Carlo's death, major technological and societal shifts occurred with the advent and growth of social media. Carlo died in the same year that Twitter and Facebook launched sites that allowed anyone with a valid e-mail address to open an account.[18] When Carlo died in 2006, only 16 percent of all Internet users in the United States used at least one social networking site, according to the Pew Research Center. By 2011, that percentage had jumped to 65 percent.[19] As a result, Carlo's story spread quickly online as enthusiastic fans in Facebook groups shared photos and updates, in different languages, about Carlo's life.

On February 15, 2013, the Catholic bishops of the Italian region of Lombardy, in whose capital, Milan, Carlo died, approved the opening of the diocesan cause for Carlo's beatification along with those of five other Servants of God: Ettore Boschini, Father Primo Mazzolari, Jean Thierry, Giovanni Cazzani, and Teresio Olivelli.*

When Carlo's cause was opened by Cardinal Angelo Scola, the archbishop of Milan, Carlo Acutis received the title Servant of God. The process began on the local level with an investigation and a collection of testimonies from those who personally knew Carlo. Typically, people are asked to testify to the exemplary life, positive influence, apostolic fruitfulness, or edifying death of a candidate for sainthood.[20]

* Among the others whose causes were opened on this date, only one was beatified before Carlo: Blessed Teresio Olivelli, a Catholic layman, was martyred by the Nazis in the Hersbruck concentration camp in 1945.

Witnesses who knew Carlo were asked to evaluate whether he lived a life of "heroic virtue". Heroic virtue includes both the theological virtues of faith, hope, and charity and the cardinal virtues of prudence, justice, temperance, and fortitude. In total, the statements and testimonies of fifty-seven witnesses were collected during the diocesan inquiry.[21]

As the first phase of Carlo's cause came to a close, the Vatican hosted a press conference about a new book and documentary film about Carlo Acutis' life.[22] The head of the Vatican Communications Department at the time made comments about Carlo that resulted in headlines around the world. Vatican spokesman Monsignor Dario Edoardo Viganò said: "Who knows if Carlo Acutis, once proclaimed blessed, might also be recognized as the patron of the Internet?"[23] He added that Carlo was "totally a child of the Web and the digital age".[24] Soon after, Italy's most-read newspaper, *Corriere della Sera*, ran an article "Carlo, Computer Genius Who Died at 15 to Be the First Blessed 2.0".

Cardinal Scola offered a Mass for the closing of the diocesan stage of Carlo's beatification cause on November 24, 2016.[25] On July 5, 2018, Pope Francis gave his approval to declare Carlo Venerable.[26] The title Venerable Servant of God means that a person either died as a martyr or that the Vatican has officially declared, as in Carlo's case, that he led a life of heroic virtue that was worthy of imitation.

Over the next year, the Vatican Dicastery for the Causes of Saints turned its attention to examining the medical evidence for the miracle attributed to Carlo's intercession. On November 14, 2019, a council convened by the Vatican for medical consultation gave a positive opinion of the miracle, acknowledging that the healing of Matheus had been "rapid, complete, and lasting" and "inexplicable in the light of current medical knowledge".

In 2024, Pope Francis recognized the second medical miracle attributed to Carlo's intercession, which made possible his canonization. The miracle involved the healing of a twenty-one-year-old Costa Rican student, Valeria Valverde, who suffered a severe head injury in a bicycle accident in Florence in 2022. After undergoing emergency surgery to relieve intracranial pressure, Valeria's condition was critical. Doctors warned her family that she could die at any moment.[27]

In desperation and faith, six days after the accident, Valeria's mother left her daughter's bedside to embark on a pilgrimage to Assisi. She left a handwritten prayer at Carlo's tomb, asking for her daughter's healing. On that same day, Valeria began to breathe on her own, defying her doctors' expectations. By the next day, she regained movement in her arms and some speech. Within ten days, she was discharged from intensive care. Medical tests revealed that the hemorrhagic right temporal cortical contusion in her brain had vanished entirely.

Valeria's recovery was so remarkable that it astonished her doctors. Contrary to medical predictions, she required only one week of physical therapy before resuming normal activities. Two months after her accident, she traveled with her mother on pilgrimage to Assisi to thank Carlo for his intercession, celebrating her complete healing—a healing inexplicable except as a miracle.

Sainthood in the Twenty-First Century

As a candidate for canonization who died in the twenty-first century, Carlo was among the first whose online correspondence could have been considered in the investigatory process, both at the local level and by the Vatican. The idea of examining someone's digital footprint is something relatively new in the centuries-old Catholic tradition of canonization. According to a former official in the Vatican Dicastery for the Causes of Saints, the Vatican has already evaluated e-mail correspondence for the causes of some religious superior generals who communicated with their provinces via e-mail. E-mails sent by a religious superior general to convents in different parts of the world, for example, could even be considered and evaluated by the Vatican as published writings. In the twentieth century, the Vatican congregation had to adapt to evaluating new types of media, including television and video recordings, particularly with the causes of Venerable Fulton Sheen and Saint Josemaría Escrivá.

Examining a candidate's digital presence is likely to be something that will necessarily become a part of the Vatican's process. One can only imagine what the investigatory process will be like for a young member of "Gen Z": the Vatican will have to dig into many text messages, e-mails, blog posts, TikTok videos, X and Instagram posts, YouTube videos, posts on old Facebook profiles, and other forms of the seemingly endless stream of electronic communication.

15

Carlo Goes Viral

At the beginning of 2020, people made plans and set goals for a new year and a new decade. Those New Year's resolutions had barely been broken when news of a viral outbreak in China began catching the attention of the world. This virus, which caused an illness called COVID-19, was spreading at an exponential rate from the first outbreak reported in Wuhan, China, in December 2019 to a new European epicenter in February 2020: Carlo's hometown of Milan.

As the news became slowly engulfed by tallies and statistics on coronavirus case counts, the Vatican made an announcement on February 22, 2020, that garnered less attention. Pope Francis had approved a miracle attributed to the intercession of Carlo Acutis. At the time, there were 1,402 confirmed cases and eleven deaths due to COVID-19 worldwide, outside of China,[1] and the word "lockdown" had no practical meaning for people's lives. Everything was about to change.

One day after the Vatican's announcement, the Archdiocese of Milan suspended all Masses, and Italian government officials imposed strict quarantine restrictions.[2] The coronavirus pandemic marked a new moment in which whole dioceses of Catholics were deprived of the Mass and the Real Presence for weeks and even months. People were told to tune in online to watch the sacrifice of the Mass via live stream, opening up an entirely new conversation on what a sacrament is and is not.

The first serious outbreak of COVID-19 in Italy was in the northern region of Lombardy, where Carlo had grown up. The situation was especially bad in Bergamo, a town about forty miles from where Carlo made his First Communion. Army trucks transported up to seventy coffins a day from Bergamo to cemeteries in other Italian cities after the local mortuaries filled up.[3]

The online phrase "to go viral"—used when something is spread widely at a rapid pace on the Internet—takes its name from the nature of a virus, which can rapidly replicate inside its host and quickly spread from person to person without the slightest touch. During the COVID-19 pandemic, remote learning and working from home forced people online as never before. And Carlo was about to go viral.

Beatification in Assisi

Carlo Acutis' beatification in Assisi in the fall of 2020 was a celebration amid Italy's "long Lent" of months of cancellations, postponements, and quarantines. The gathering took place against all odds at a time between Italy's two major national lockdowns. Most foreign tourists, including Americans, were not allowed to travel to Italy.

Despite the limitations, the bishop of Assisi saw the potential for Carlo's beatification to be an evangelizing force for young people. Archbishop Domenico Sorrentino decided that the diocese would spread out the celebration over a few weeks of smaller-scale liturgies, youth rallies, and exhibitions, as well as some virtual events. During this time, Catholic churches throughout Assisi offered additional hours of adoration of the Blessed Sacrament each day in honor of Carlo's devotion to the Real Presence. A life-size cardboard cutout of Carlo standing with a giant monstrance containing the Eucharist could be seen in front of many churches in Assisi. The Acutis family's exhibition on eucharistic miracles was displayed in the Cathedral of San Rufino. At an evening youth vigil, a crowd of pilgrims gathered outside Assisi's Basilica of Saint Mary of the Angels while priests heard confessions inside.

Days before the beatification, the Italian government had announced a nationwide medical mask requirement for anyone walking outdoors. This meant that the many Franciscans walking the cobblestone streets of the medieval city of Assisi now donned a new item along with their brown habits—a mint-green face mask. Smartly dressed Italian police officers found new vigor for their work in enforcing the emergency decree. Rolling down the window of a police car, an officer called out to a Franciscan friar, "*Frate, mascarina, per favore*", urging the friar to pull up his mask to cover his nose. Despite all this, Italians descended on the city of Assisi in cars and trains for Carlo's beatification.

The beatification Mass took place in the Basilica of Saint Francis of Assisi on October 10, 2020. Masked pilgrims spread out in front of the basilica and throughout the piazzas in Assisi to watch the Mass on large screens, as only a limited number of people were allowed inside. Carlo's parents processed behind a relic of their son's heart during the Mass. Two other special family members also attended the beatification: Carlo's younger twin siblings, Michele and Francesca, who were born four years after Carlo died.[4] The twins were ten years old when they watched their older brother raised to the altars.

An apostolic letter from Pope Francis, read aloud in the thirteenth-century basilica during the ceremony, declared that Carlo Acutis' feast could be celebrated locally each year on October 12, the anniversary of his death. Cardinal Agostino Vallini, the pontifical legate for the Basilica of Saint Francis, presided over the Mass and hailed Carlo as a model of how young people can use technology at the service of the Gospel. "Since he was a child . . . [Carlo] had his gaze turned to Jesus. Love for the Eucharist was the foundation that kept alive his relationship with God. He often said, 'The Eucharist is my highway to heaven'", Cardinal Vallini said in his homily.[5] "Carlo felt a strong need to help people discover that God is close to us and that it is beautiful to be with him to enjoy his friendship and his grace."

Mattia Pastorelli, one of Carlo's childhood friends, commented: "Having a friend who is about to become a saint [evokes] a very strange emotion."[6] Pastorelli, who met Carlo when they were both around the age of five, recalled fond memories of playing on the computer with Carlo. "I watched him while he was programming websites. . . . He was truly an incredible talent", he added.[7]

Carlo's beatification drew an estimated three thousand people to Assisi on the day of the main Mass. Thousands more tuned in to the online live stream of the event. According to Google Trends, there was also a spike in Google searches for the term "eucharistic miracles" during the weeks surrounding Carlo's beatification, with the number of searches increasing tenfold from September 2020 to October 2020.[8] What Carlo had longed for in his lifetime was finally coming true after his death: more and more people were learning about eucharistic miracles and the Real Presence of Jesus in the Eucharist.

On the day after the beatification, Pope Francis said that Blessed Carlo's life provided a witness for young people that true happiness is found when one puts God first. Speaking from the window of the Apostolic Palace to pilgrims gathered in Saint Peter's Square for his Sunday Angelus address, the pope called Carlo "a fifteen-year-old boy in love with the Eucharist". Pope Francis said: "He did not settle into comfortable inaction, but grasped the needs of his time because in the weakest he saw the face of Christ. His witness shows today's young people that true happiness is found by putting God first and serving Him in our brothers, especially the least."[9]

Carlo's Tomb

More than forty-one thousand people visited Carlo's tomb during the nineteen-day celebration of his beatification, according to the Diocese of Assisi.[10] The boy's tomb is located inside the Church of Saint Mary Major, which served as Assisi's cathedral until the eleventh century. The place where he is buried is also known in English as the Sanctuary of the Renunciation because it marks the spot where a young Saint Francis of Assisi is said to have cast off his rich clothes in favor of a poor habit to give himself entirely to God.* The church itself has a special place in Pope Francis' heart.† He has called the Sanctuary of the Renunciation "a precious place where young people can be aided in the discernment of their vocations".[11]

An entrance to the church is marked by large images of Carlo, including a cardboard cutout of him standing with a backpack beside a giant eucharistic monstrance. Yet rather than leading directly to his tomb, this entrance offers first a

* The place where Carlo is buried is called the Santuario della Spogliazione in Italian.

† In a letter written in 2017, Pope Francis recalled his time spent praying in the church during his emotional first visit to Assisi after taking the name Francis.

direct aisle leading to a golden tabernacle below a historic fresco of Jesus on the cross. Carlo, who called the Eucharist "my highway to heaven", would have liked this setup. Anyone who wants to approach his tomb must first approach the Eucharist. A series of ropes set up in the church leads pilgrims from the tabernacle to Carlo's tomb in the back right corner of the church.

A Saint in Sneakers

Visitors to Assisi who enter the Sanctuary of the Renunciation can see, through a viewing glass on his tomb, the first millennial to be beatified in the Catholic Church, dressed in jeans, a track jacket, and Nike tennis shoes and holding a rosary.* Etched in the center of the viewing glass on the tomb is the IHS monogram encircled by sun-like beams—an ancient symbol for the name Jesus Christ. These three letters were often written on the tombs of Christians in the early Church. Saint Ignatius of Loyola later adopted it when he founded the Jesuit Order.[12]

Illuminated above the tomb, thirty mosaic panels in various polygonal shapes illustrate scenes and themes from Carlo's life carved into white stone.[13] The mosaic includes some images one would expect of a Catholic saint—Carlo is depicted in eucharistic adoration, praying the Rosary, and receiving Communion—yet other panels are unique.† One

* After Carlo's beatification, Archbishop Sorrentino extended the time available for public viewing of Carlo's body to October 19, 2020, due to the number of people who wished to pray at Carlo's tomb. Following this date, a panel was placed over the viewing glass on the tomb until June 1, 2022, when Carlo's tomb was permanently reopened for public veneration.

† Panels include illustrations of Carlo swimming with dolphins, Carlo playing the saxophone, and Carlo beside the book *The Little Prince* by

panel shows Carlo surrounded by his two cats and four dogs. Another shows the twenty-first-century teen at the Last Supper, reclining against Jesus, like Saint John, the beloved disciple.[14] And in what must surely be a first for the Catholic Church, a panel shows Carlo typing at his computer, surrounded by the brand icons of Wikipedia, Internet Explorer, Google, Firefox, Facebook, Pinterest,‡ Safari, Twitter, Instagram, and YouTube.[15]

"For the first time in history we will see a saint dressed in jeans, sneakers, and a sweater", said Father Carlos Acácio Gonçalves Ferreira, the rector of the Sanctuary of the Renunciation in Assisi, during the week of the tomb's opening. "This is a great message for us, we can feel holiness not as a distant thing but as something very much within everyone's reach because the Lord is the Lord of everyone."[16]

Father Boniface Lopez, a Franciscan Capuchin based at Assisi's Sanctuary of the Renunciation, noted that many people who visited Carlo's tomb also took advantage of the opportunity to go to Confession, which was offered in many languages throughout the days when Carlo's body was first made visible for veneration. "Many people are coming to see Carlo to ask for his blessing . . . also many young people; they come for confessions. They come because they want to change their lives and they want to come near God and really experience God."[17] Father Lopez also encountered many religious sisters and priests who had come on pilgrimage to pray at Carlo's tomb. "Religious come here

---

Antoine de Saint-Exupéry; Carlo is also shown standing in front of different locations, including New York, the Milan Cathedral, London, Fátima, Lourdes, Mont San Michel, and in front of his home parish, giving money to the poor.

‡ Note that some of these companies did not exist until after Carlo died.

to ask his blessing to help them to cultivate a greater love for the Eucharist'', he said.

Next Step: Sainthood

One of the many people who tuned in virtually to Carlo's beatification was thirty-four-year-old Melissa Guerrero, who woke up early in her hospital room to follow the ceremony via live stream one day after being treated in the emergency room. Due to a severe vitamin A deficiency, Guerrero found herself gradually going blind in both eyes. Mentally, physically, and emotionally exhausted, she began to pray, through tears, for Carlo's intercession when she felt a reassuring presence next to her hospital bed.

Watching the beatification online also brought her to tears, but this time they were tears of joy: "I looked up at the . . . screen just as he was being declared a blessed. My eyes welled up as I saw his face: the first image I'd been able to see since I'd lost my eyesight months earlier. I broke down in tears as I described his picture to my mom; to make sure I was seeing it correctly. I was."[18] Melissa, who has since recovered more of her eyesight, is dedicated to doing everything she can to help other visually impaired Catholics and to encourage devotion to Blessed Carlo. She said: "Mark my words; Blessed Carlo Acutis will become a canonized saint someday."[19]

16

What Carlo Can Teach Gen Z

The Internet age in which Carlo spent his childhood is no doubt different from what kids experience today. Carlo did not live to see the social media explosion or the widespread use of smartphones that have transformed society. He died in 2006 before the launch of the iPhone or Instagram and when the TikTok boom was still more than a decade away. Carlo barely lived to see the first-ever cat video uploaded to the Internet. Yet as a heavenly intercessor, he is still plugged in to the increasingly online lives of his fellow millennials and the younger generations as an advocate and a guide.

Pope Francis has presented Carlo Acutis as a witness of holiness in a digital world in which young people are consistently tempted to "self-absorption, isolation and empty pleasure".[1] In a fifty-page letter addressed to "all Christian young people" called *Christus vivit* (Christ lives), Pope Francis wrote:

> I remind you of the good news we received as a gift on the morning of the resurrection: that in all the dark or painful situations that we mentioned, there is a way out. For example, it is true that the digital world can expose you to the risk of self-absorption, isolation and empty pleasure. But don't forget that there are young people even there who show creativity and even genius. That was the case with the Venerable Carlo Acutis.

> Carlo was well aware that the whole apparatus of communications, advertising, and social networking can be used to lull us, to make us addicted to consumerism and buying the latest thing on the market, obsessed with our free time, caught up in negativity. Yet he knew how to use the new communications technology to transmit the Gospel, to communicate values and beauty.
>
> Carlo didn't fall into the trap. He saw that many young people, wanting to be different, really end up being like everyone else, running after whatever the powerful set before them with the mechanisms of consumerism and distraction. In this way they do not bring forth the gifts the Lord has given them; they do not offer the world those unique personal talents that God has given to each of them. As a result, Carlo said, "Everyone is born as an original, but many people end up dying as photocopies". Don't let that happen to you!
>
> Don't let them rob you of hope and joy, or drug you into becoming a slave to their interests. Dare to be more, because who you are is more important than any possession. What good are possessions or appearances? You can become what God your Creator knows you are, if only you realize that you are called to something greater. Ask the help of the Holy Spirit and confidently aim for the great goal of holiness. In this way, you will not be a photocopy. You will be fully yourself.[2]

Pope Francis pointed to Carlo as a witness that young people today are "called to something greater" than endless scrolling on a smartphone or sitting in front of a laptop.

Carlo Acutis loved computers, but he did not lose himself in an online world, spending all day gaming without leaving the house. He remained firmly planted in concrete reality through his daily interactions with people and through the sacraments—the tangible signs that "make present efficaciously the grace that they signify".[3] While it is true that certain technological limitations in Carlo's day forced boundaries on the amount of time he could spend online, teens today can still learn from how he prioritized the sacraments, which helped to guide him to make better choices and to make his time online fruitful.

Gen Z and Digital Addiction

The generation born immediately after Carlo's millennial generation grew up when cell phones were already ubiquitous. Generation Z, also called iGen or just Gen Z, were born after 1995 and are true digital natives, never having experienced a world without the Web.[4] It can be said that smartphones are the biggest difference in their lives when compared with previous generations, and these small devices are having a huge impact on Gen Z kids. Two out of three teens in the United States owned an iPhone in 2015,[5] less than ten years after Apple first introduced the product, which was released one year after Carlo died. By 2022, 87 percent of U.S. teens surveyed owned an iPhone.[6]

According to Jean Twenge, the author of *iGen*, the average teen checks his phone more than eighty times a day, and many teens sleep with their phones within arm's reach.[7] A study published in 2022 found that before the COVID-19 pandemic, nine- and ten-year-old kids spent on average nearly four hours in front of a screen each day.[8] Young social media users are "constantly in search of likes and positive comments on their pages, with the persistent pressure to post sexy and revealing photos", Twenge said.[9]

Pope Francis has warned against cell phone and social media addiction. The pope observed that addiction to digital media "impoverishes human relationships".[10] Studies show that there are even worse dangers: teen suicide and depression, porn exposure among kids, teens sending nude photos to each other, and cyberbullying. Twenge's research has documented how "teen depression and suicide rates have skyrocketed since 2011", the year she pinpoints as the moment when most Americans began to own smartphones.[11] According to the U.S. Centers for Disease Control and Prevention (CDC), the suicide rate increased by nearly 60 percent between 2007 and 2018 for people aged ten to twenty-four years old.[12] And this was before the COVID-19 pandemic drastically changed young people's habits and opportunities for social interaction. Twenge found back in 2017 that "eighth graders who are heavy users of social media increase their risk of depression by 27 percent while those who play sports, attend religious services, or even do homework decrease their risk significantly".[13] She also found that "teens who spent more than three hours a day on electronic devices are 35 percent more likely to have at least one suicide risk factor".[14]

Neil Postman wrote a book in 1985 with the prophetic title *Amusing Ourselves to Death.*[15] Decades later, there is perhaps no better description of the prevalence of binge-watching and of the screen-time-obsessed youth culture in the West. Middle school students who dedicated some of their time to religious practice, reading books, and sports were more likely to report that they were happy than those who spent more hours on the Internet, social media, texting, gaming, or video chat, according to Twenge, who found that eighth-grade students who spent six hours a week or more on social media were 47 percent more likely to say that they were unhappy.[16]

For those who are concerned that the amount of time

they themselves spend on smartphones, social media, or online gaming is excessive, the Catholic Church offers a long tradition of fasting practices to draw from. The Christian practice of fasting is the training of one's willpower, reordering desires according to proper priorities. This is not easy, but one is not asked to do it all alone. Fasting during Lent, for example, is meant to heighten one's awareness of the need for God.

Pope Francis has proposed that the forty-day season of Lent can be "a propitious time" to resist the temptation to pick up the smartphone and to "cultivate instead a more integral form of human communication made up of 'authentic encounters,' face to face and in person".[17] The practice of fasting, whether it be from food or a smartphone, should always be accompanied by prayer. Prayer to the saints to ask for their intercession can be a powerful means to break the chains of social media or Internet addiction. Carlo Acutis, who was fascinated by computers and saw their potential good while maintaining his priorities of love of God and love of neighbor above all, is a fantastic Saint to call upon for assistance in limiting harmful digital-media usage.

Generation Z is more likely than any generation in the modern age to grow up being raised by religiously unaffiliated parents.[18] And fewer members of Gen Z practice a religion compared with Carlo's millennial generation. Twenge found in her research that Gen Z is "actually less spiritual as well as being less religious". One out of three eighteen- to twenty-four-year-olds said in 2016 that they "did not believe in God", and more than one in four young adults said that they "never prayed".[19] Carlo knew what it felt like to be living out a countercultural faith in an increasingly less religious world. One in three millennials told Pew Research Center as young adults that they had no religious affiliation.[20]

Carlo's example has the potential to show the generation on the verge of "the most severe mental health crisis for young people in decades"[21] that true joy and fulfillment are found in Christ's life-giving love and divine mercy.

Young People Calling on Carlo

Many people have already found inspiration from Carlo as an example of "what holiness looks like in the twenty-first century". This is what Cecilia Cicone from Delaware told Catholic News Agency when she was twenty-five years old: "Carlo puts flesh on what a saint who plays video games and goes on the internet looks like. He challenges me to examine my conscience and say, 'Ok, I'm called to be a saint who uses the internet too. Am I using it to make God's love known?'" She added: "With the beatification of Carlo Acutis, for the first time, I experience the peace and joy of recognizing that I, too, can be a saint of the twenty-first century. It's not a hypothetical anymore."[22]

Maria Roberts, a girl in her twenties who worked as a computer programmer, said that she saw Carlo as an example of how to use the Internet for good:

> It is important for us as Catholics to think about how technology can be used for good and for evangelization, and not as a way to take advantage of others or demoralize young people. There is so much good to be done and so much suffering nowadays—young people should know that their talents can be used for God's glory in many ways through our technological advances.[23]

As Ani, a member of Gen Z from Texas, put it: "I feel like Carlo [is] maybe the first saint I've seen that's had an actually normal, human, attainable way to [live an extraordinarily holy life].''[24]

U.S. bishops have also turned to Carlo Acutis as an intercessor, naming him the patron of the first year of a National Eucharistic Revival.[25] The bishops launched the revival in 2022 after a survey found that three-quarters of Catholics under forty in the United States did not believe Church teaching about the Real Presence of Christ in the Eucharist.[26] The bishops hope that Carlo's story—along with that of the revival's other patron saint, Manuel Gonzalez Garcia—can help to awaken Catholics, especially younger ones, to the Lord's presence among us.

The witness of Carlo's life is spreading, not just in the United States but all around the world.* Father Adrian Sadowski, the diocesan youth chaplain in northeast Poland, was looking for a way to inspire young people who consider themselves ''spiritual but not religious'' to see the importance of the sacraments. With this in mind, the Polish priest contacted the Vatican with the hope of obtaining a first-class relic of Carlo Acutis for his diocese, which he eventually obtained and installed in the cathedral in the Diocese of Ełk. Father Adrian said:

> In today's world, many young people ask questions about faith and the Church. Many say, ''God, yes, but the Church as an institution, no'' and some doubt eternity. Sometimes it is difficult for them to understand that the Church ''is a hospital for sinners'' and only in it can one meet the living God in sacramental action. Blessed Carlo makes us aware of this. . . . In today's reality, when the everyday life of young

* World Youth Day in Lisbon, Portugal, featured Carlo as a patron saint with the hope that more young people will discover this friendly intercessor and be inspired by his witness of a holy life.

> people moved to the internet . . . the Church gives us a Blessed who used this means for evangelization.[27]

Next-Gen Saints

The digital revolution has brought about societal shifts at such a rapid pace that Christians are still grappling with how best to live out their faith in a brave new world of laptops, smartphones, and "virtual communities" on social media. Looking forward, Carlo Acutis will hopefully be not only the first millennial saint but the first of many future generations of Catholic saints who reached the heights of holiness while using computers and other new technologies.

Carlo shows that it is not necessary to unplug completely from the modern world in order to remain faithful. It is possible to use the information superhighway to spread the Gospel, just as the early Christians used Roman roads. And there is no "one size fits" all when it comes to how Christians should approach technology. As Carlo reminds us, no saint is a "photocopy", but all are originals.

No matter what new innovations or distractions the world churns out next, the essentials of a life of faith remain unchanging. Amid endless information, God's word remains. In the face of life's challenges, hope remains. At the end of life, love remains. Each person has a limited amount of time on Earth. Carlo lived only 5,640 days,[28] yet he tried his best to make as many of them as possible days on which he was united to the Real Presence of Christ through the Eucharist, the "source and summit" of the Christian life, and this became his "highway to heaven".

Prayer to Saint Carlo Acutis

O God, our Father,
we thank you for giving us Saint Carlo Acutis
as a role model for young people
and as a message of love for all.
You made him burn with love
for your Son, Jesus,
and taught him to treat the Eucharist
as his "Highway to Heaven".
You gave him Mary as a beloved Mother,
and through the Rosary, you inspired him
to sing of her tenderness.
Hear his prayer on our behalf.
Watch especially over the poor,
whom he loved and treasured so much.
Through his example, show us how
to use technology responsibly
not for selfish ends, but for your kingdom.
Grant me also, through his intercession,
the grace that I need . . . [*state your intention*]
Give us the joy of knowing
that Carlo, together with all your saints,
smiles radiantly on us from heaven
to the glory of your name.

Amen.

Acknowledgments

Heartfelt thanks to my first readers, Bennett Rawicki, Chris Wolfe, Audrey Lenahan, and Melanie Wilcox. Not many people can brag that their bridal party has such a talent for manuscript editing. I am incredibly grateful to Ellen Loesel, Rajesh Mohur, and Father Roberto Gazzaniga for sharing their personal stories, and to Antonia Salzano Acutis for all she has done to help us know better her remarkable son. Thank you to the great team at Ignatius Press, especially Thomas Jacobi, Nora Malone, Laura Shoemaker, and all who helped to bring this biography to life. Special thanks to Gail Gavin for her crucial feedback and edits. Thanks also to Michael White and Anthony Dalby for their technical expertise on computer coding, to fellow writer and friend M.G. Prezioso for cheering me on, and to Father Michael Baggot, Father Joseph Hudson, and Monsignor Thomas Cook for wise advice and spiritual encouragement during the writing process. I cannot fail to thank Luke Coppen, the first person who encouraged me to write a biography of Blessed Carlo. And above all, I would like to thank my beloved husband, Miguel, without whose love, support, and patience this book would not have been possible.

Notes

1. Global "Influencer for God"

[1] Ellen Loesel, interview by author via telephone, September 19, 2021.

[2] "We know that in everything God works for good with those who love him, who are called according to his purpose" (Rom 8:28).

[3] Comparison of Google search data for "Carlo Acutis" and "Pope Francis" in October 2020, Google Trends, https://tinyurl.com/3pa4cf22.

[4] Google search data for "eucharistic miracles" in 2006 to 2022, Google Trends, https://trends.google.com/trends/explore?date=2006-01-01%202022-12-01&q=Eucharistic%20miracles.

[5] Salvatore Cernuzio, "Carlo Acutis beato, la mamma: 'Mio figlio un influencer positivo per tanti giovani di oggi'", *La Stampa*, June 16, 2020, https://tinyurl.com/hr9jfzzw.

[6] Larry Greenemeier, "Remembering the Day the World Wide Web Was Born," *Scientific American*, March 12, 2009, https://scientificamerican.com/article/day-the-web-was-born/.

[7] Nicola Gori, *Eucaristia: La mia autostrada per il cielo. Biografia di Carlo Acutis (1991–2006)*, 8th ed. (Cinisello Balsamo [Milan]: San Paolo, 2007), 132. Throughout this book, unless otherwise noted, all quotations from Italian sources were translated into English by the author.

[8] Giorgio Maria Carbone, *Originali o fotocopie?* (Bologna: Edizioni Studio Domenicano, 2021), 70, quoting Congregatio de Causis Sanctorum, *Mediolanensis beatificationis et canonizationis servi Dei Carlo Acutis, Christifidelis laici (1991–2006): Positio super vita, virtutibus et fama sanctitatis* (Romae, 2017), 316.

[9] Gori, *Eucaristia*, 87.

2. A Great Grace

[1] Antonia Salzano Acutis and Paolo Rodari, *Il segreto di mio figlio. Perché Carlo Acutis è considerato un santo* (Milan: Piemme, 2021), 102.

[2] Giorgio Maria Carbone, *Originali o fotocopie?* (Bologna: Edizioni Studio Domenicano, 2021), 17, quoting Congregatio de Causis Sanctorum, *Mediolanensis beatificationis et canonizationis servi Dei Carlo Acutis, Christifidelis laici (1991–2006): Positio super vita, virtutibus et fama sanctitatis* (Romae, 2017), 295 (hereafter cited as *Positio*).

[3] Gian Guido Vecchi, "Carlo Acutis, fede e internet: Il 15enne Milanese sarà il primo beato dei millennials", *Corriere della Sera*, October 9, 2020, 27.

[4] Salzano Acutis and Rodari, *Il segreto*, 88.

[5] Carbone, *Originali o fotocopie*, 17.

[6] Andrea Acutis. Curriculum Vitae. "Governance," Vittoria Assicurazioni. https://www.vittoriaassicurazioni.com/Allegati/Governance/PDF_GOVERNANCE_ENG/Corporate%20bodies/board%20of%20Directors/Andrea%20Acutis.pdf.

[7] Salzano Acutis and Rodari, *Il segreto*, 90.

[8] Carlo weighed exactly 3.5 kilograms. Antonia Salzano Acutis and Paolo Rodari, *Il segreto di mio figlio. Perché Carlo Acutis è considerato un santo* (Milan: Piemme, 2021).

[9] "Andrea Acutis".

[10] Her full name, Luana Pennino, was published in Carbone, *Originali o fotocopie*, 35.

[11] Salzano Acutis and Rodari, *Il segreto*, 118.

[12] *Catechism of the Catholic Church* (CCC), no. 1241.

[13] Salzano Acutis and Rodari, *Il segreto*, 89.

[14] After Carlo's death, Andrea Acutis took over as president of Vittoria Insurance.

[15] Beata's full name, Beata Sperczynska, was published in the following sources: Cardinal Marcello Semeraro's introduction to Michele Munno, in *La scala più corta per salire in cielo. Rosario con il beato Carlo Acutis* (Ancona, Italy: Editrice Shalom, 2021); Archbishop Domenico Sorrentino, *Originali, non fotocopie. Carlo Acutis e Francesco d'Assisi* (Perugia, Italy: Edizioni Francescane Italiane, 2019), 48, quoting *Positio*, 150–54; Carbone, *Originali o fotocopie*, 74.

[16] Salzano Acutis and Rodari, *Il segreto*, 111.

[17] Stefano Lorenzetto, "Antonia Salzano: 'Il miracolo di Carlo Acutis, mio figlio, morto 15enne di leucemia: un santo per il web'", *Corriere della Sera*, September 4, 2020, https://tinyurl.com/2p9bwn9p.

[18] David A. Andelman, "Pope Gets Big Welcome in Poland, Offers Challenge to the Authorities", *New York Times*, June 3, 1979, https://nytimes.com/1979/06/03/archives/pope-gets-big-welcome-in-poland-offers-challenge-to-the-authorities.html.

[19] Carbone, *Originali o fotocopie*, 18, quoting *Positio*, 295.

[20] Semeraro, introduction to Munno, "La scala più corta", 6.

[21] Ibid.

[22] John Paul II, apostolic letter *Rosarium Virginis Mariae* (October 16, 2002), no. 2.

[23] Carbone, *Originali o fotocopie*, 150, quoting *Positio*, 151.

[24] Carbone, *Originali o fotocopie*, 135, quoting *Positio*, 154.

[25] Carbone, *Originali o fotocopie*, 150, quoting *Positio*, 152.

[26] *I Am with You: A Documentary on Carlo Acutis*, a Cristiana video and EWTN production, 2021, 35:01, https://ondemand.ewtn.com/free/Home/Play/381-373197.

[27] Carbone, *Originali o fotocopie*, 18, quoting *Positio*, 295.

[28] Carbone, *Originali o fotocopie*, 134.

[29] Carbone, *Originali o fotocopie*, 207, quoting *Positio*, 297.

[30] Carbone, *Originali o fotocopie*, 134, quoting *Positio*, 296.

[31] Ary Waldir Ramos Diaz, "The Mother of Venerable Carlo Acutis Says He Was Her Little Savior", Aleteia, May 12, 2019, https://aleteia.org/2019/05/12/the-mother-of-venerable-carlo-acutis-says-he-was-her-little-savior/.

[32] Lorenzetto, "Il miracolo di Carlo Acutis".

[33] Salzano Acutis and Rodari, *Il segreto*, 113.

[34] *I Am with You.* Antonia used the same phrase in her testimony to the Vatican. See Sorrentino, *Carlo Acutis e Francesco d'Assisi*, 48, quoting *Positio*, 299.

3. A Nineties Kid

[1] Michael Dimock, "Defining Generations: Where Millennials End and Generation Z Begins", Pew Research Center, April 21, 2022,

https://pewresearch.org/fact-tank/2019/01/17/where-millennials-end-and-generation-z-begins/.

[2] John B. Horrigan, "Consumption of Information Goods and Services in the U.S.", Pew Research Center, November 23, 2003, https://pewresearch.org/internet/2003/11/23/consumption-of-information-goods-and-services-in-the-u-s/.

[3] Antonia Salzano Acutis and Paolo Rodari, *Il segreto di mio figlio. Perché Carlo Acutis è considerato un santo* (Milan: Piemme, 2021), 76–77.

[4] Dicastery for the Causes of Saints, Decree on the Virtues of Servant of God Carlo Acutis (July 5, 2018), http://causesanti.va/it/santi-e-beati/carlo-acutis.html.

[5] Salzano Acutis and Rodari, *Il segreto*, 111.

[6] Ibid., 182.

[7] Courtney Mares, "Blessed Carlo Acutis' 30th Birthday Celebrated by Parishes across World", Catholic News Agency, May 3, 2021, https://catholicnewsagency.com/news/247504/blessed-carlo-acutis-30th-birthday-celebrated-by-parishes-across-world.

[8] Salzano Acutis and Rodari, *Il segreto*, 71.

[9] Teena and Aditya Ayyagari, "Talk to Rajesh Mohur about Blessed Carlo Acutis", YouTube video, 1:30:35, November 13, 2020, https://youtu.be/WxQ6MAwqIPQ.

[10] The Tommaseo Institute began in 1906 with two hundred students. "La storia del Tommaseo inizia nel 1906", Istituto Marcelline Tommaseo, http://www.marcellinetommaseo.it/chi-siamo/.

[11] Salzano Acutis and Rodari, *Il segreto*, 169.

[12] Ibid., 172.

[13] Ibid., 189.

[14] Ibid., 190.

[15] Carbone, *Originali o fotocopie*, 155, quoting *Positio*, 203.

[16] Carbone, *Originali o fotocopie*, 156, quoting *Positio*, 203.

[17] Will Conquer, *Carlo Acutis: A Millennial in Paradise* (Manchester, N.H.: Sophia Institute Press, 2021), 20.

[18] Salzano Acutis and Rodari, *Il segreto*, 55.

4. Highway to Heaven

[1] Will Conquer, *Carlo Acutis: A Millennial in Paradise* (Manchester, N.H.: Sophia Institute Press, 2021), 97.

[2] Giorgio Maria Carbone, *Originali o fotocopie?* (Bologna: Edizioni Studio Domenicano, 2021), 70, quoting Congregatio de Causis Sanctorum, *Mediolanensis beatificationis et canonizationis servi Dei Carlo Acutis, Christifidelis laici (1991–2006): Positio super vita, virtutibus et fama sanctitatis* (Romae, 2017), 316 (hereafter cited as *Positio*).

[3] Carbone, *Originali o fotocopie*, 75, quoting *Positio*, 151.

[4] Paola Bergamini, "Nothing More Than Lifting Your Gaze", *Traces*, February 2014, http://archivio.traces-cl.com/2014/02/nothing more.html.

[5] *I Am with You: A Documentary on Carlo Acutis*, a Cristiana video and EWTN production, 2021, 35:01, https://ondemand.ewtn.com/free/Home/Play/381-373197.

[6] Nicola Gori, *Eucaristia: La mia autostrada per il cielo. Biografia di Carlo Acutis (1991–2006)*, 8th ed. (Cinisello Balsamo [Milan]: San Paolo, 2007), 105. The religious superior is named in Antonia Salzano Acutis and Paolo Rodari, *Il segreto di mio figlio. Perché Carlo Acutis è considerato un santo* (Milan: Piemme, 2021), 257.

[7] Gori, *Eucaristia*, 101, 106.

[8] Carbone, *Originali o fotocopie*, 82, quoting *Positio*, 297.

[9] "Il mio programma di vita è quello di essere sempre unito a Gesù." Carbone, *Originali o fotocopie*, 79, quoting *Positio*, 293.

[10] Salzano Acutis and Rodari, *Il segreto*, 278.

[11] Alberto Friso, "Carlo Acutis, un piccolo salvatore", *Messaggero di Sant'Antonio*, January 21, 2023, https://messaggerosantantonio.it/content/carlo-acutis-un-piccolo-salvatore.

[12] Carbone, *Originali o fotocopie*, 137, quoting *Positio*, 117.

[13] Carbone, *Originali o fotocopie*, 110, quoting *Positio*, 316.

[14] Salzano Acutis and Rodari, *Il segreto*, 285.

[15] Gori, *Eucaristia*, 92.

[16] "Diocesi di Milano, struttura e organismi", Chiesa di Milano (Archdiocese of Milan), https://www.chiesadimilano.it/informazioni-generali.

[17] Marco Navoni, "Rito Ambrosiano. La centralità dell'opera di Sant'Ambrogio per la Chiesa di Milano," *L'Osservatore Romano*, September 29, 2002, LaParola, https://www.laparola.it/rito-ambrosiano/rito-ambrosiano-la-centralita-dellopera-di-santambrogio-per-la-chiesa-di-milano/.

[18] *I Am with You*, https://ondemand.ewtn.com/free/Home/Play/381-373197.

[19] Ibid.

[20] Gori, *Eucaristia*, 92.

[21] Carbone, *Originali o fotocopie*, 36, quoting *Positio*, 276.

[22] Carbone, *Originali o fotocopie*, 36, quoting *Positio*, 276, 279.

[23] Gori, *Eucaristia*, 123.

[24] Carbone, *Originali o fotocopie*, 119, quoting *Positio*, 317.

[25] Salzano Acutis and Rodari, *Il segreto*, 116.

[26] Ibid.

[27] Carbone, *Originali o fotocopie*, 70, quoting *Positio*, 316.

[28] *CCC* 2837, quoting Saint Ignatius of Antioch, *Ad Eph.* 20, 2 (*PG* 5, 661).

[29] Carbone, *Originali o fotocopie*, 74, quoting *Positio*, 299.

[30] Carbone, *Originali o fotocopie*, 75, quoting *Positio*, 278.

[31] Carbone, *Originali o fotocopie*, 72, quoting *Positio*, 316.

[32] Carbone, *Originali o fotocopie*, 105, quoting *Positio*, 316, 524. Antonia attributed this quotation to Carlo in her testimony to the Vatican Dicastery for the Causes of Saints.

[33] Carbone, *Originali o fotocopie*, 103–4, quoting *Positio*, 316, 317, 524.

[34] Carbone, *Originali o fotocopie*, 92, quoting *Positio*, 291.

5. From Hinduism to Catholicism

[1] Giorgio Maria Carbone, *Originali o fotocopie?* (Bologna: Edizioni Studio Domenicano, 2021), 87, quoting Congregatio de Causis Sanctorum, *Mediolanensis beatificationis et canonizationis servi Dei Carlo Acutis, Christifidelis laici (1991–2006): Positio super vita, virtutibus et fama sanctitatis* (Romae, 2017), 171 (hereafter cited as *Positio*).

[2] Carbone, *Originali o fotocopie*, 87.

[3] Carbone, *Originali o fotocopie*, 164, quoting *Positio*, 170.

[4] Mohur, interview by author. Rajesh also said: "It was Carlo's enthusiasm, his explanations, and his teachings that gave me the desire to become a Christian and to ask for Baptism." Carbone, *Originali o fotocopie*, 164, quoting *Positio*, 166.

[5] Carbone, *Originali o fotocopie*, 45, quoting *Positio*, 291.

[6] Carbone, *Originali o fotocopie*, 31, quoting *Positio*, 174.

[7] Carbone, *Originali o fotocopie*, 138, quoting *Positio*, 172.

[8] Carbone, *Originali o fotocopie*, 31, quoting *Positio*, 174.

[9] Carbone, *Originali o fotocopie*, 162, quoting *Positio*, 173.

6. Information Superhighway

[1] Antonia Salzano Acutis and Paolo Rodari, *Il segreto di mio figlio. Perché Carlo Acutis è considerato un santo* (Milan: Piemme, 2021), 244.

[2] Ibid., 244–45.

[3] John Paul II, Act of Entrustment to Mary, Vatican, October 8, 2000.

[4] Giampiero Rossi, "Carlo, genio del computer morto a 15 anni: Sarà il primo beato 2.0", *Corriere della Sera*, November 22, 2016, https://milano.corriere.it/notizie/cronaca/16_novembre_23/carlo-genio-computersara-primo-beato-20-dd621f1c-b0f5-11e6-b55d-c69c2623ee72.shtml.

[5] Philip Whiteside, "The Saint of the Internet Age", Sky News, 2020, https://news.sky.com/story/internet-saint-carlo-acutis-how-a-london-born-teenager-may-be-the-first-millennial-to-be-canonised-12170390.

[6] "A Beginner's Guide to Programming Languages", IT Hare, http://ithare.com/a-beginners-guide-to-programming-languages/.

[7] Salzano Acutis and Rodari, *Il segreto*, 185.

[8] Marcelo Tenorio, "Caríssimos divulgadores de Carlo Acutis", *Carlo Acutis, O Anjo da Juventude* (blog), November 4, 2012, http://carloacutisbr.blogspot.com/2012/11/mensagem-aos-divulgadores-de-carlo.html.

[9] Salzano Acutis and Rodari, *Il segreto*, 185.

[10] Sabrina Ferrisi, "Carlo Acutis 'Always Lived in the Presence of God'", *National Catholic Register*, June 27, 2020, https://ncregister.com/features/carlo-acutis-always-lived-in-the-presence-of-god. Ferrisi notes that Carlo also liked to use Photoshop.

[11] Nicola Gori, *Eucaristia: La mia autostrada per il cielo. Biografia di Carlo Acutis (1991–2006)*, 8th ed. (Cinisello Balsamo [Milan]: San Paolo, 2007), 58.

[12] Jean M. Twenge, *iGen* (New York: Atria Books, 2017), 5.

[13] "Motorola T720 with New Verizon Wireless Get It Now Service Helps Consumers Get Busy in Full Color", Verizon News Center, Verizon Wireless, September 23, 2002, https://www.verizon.com/about/news/press-releases/motorola-t720-new-verizon-wireless-get-it-now-service-helps-consumers-get-busy-full-color; Twenge, *iGen*, 5.

[14] Rajesh Mohur, interview by author, Milan, Italy, August 3, 2021.

[15] Giorgio Maria Carbone, *Originali o fotocopie?* (Bologna: Edizioni Studio Domenicano, 2021), 187, quoting Congregatio de Causis Sanctorum, *Mediolanensis beatificationis et canonizationis servi Dei Carlo Acutis, Christifidelis laici (1991–2006): Positio super vita, virtutibus et fama sanctitatis* (Romae, 2017), 176 (hereafter cited as *Positio*).

[16] Carbone, *Originali o fotocopie*, 187, quoting *Positio*, 171–72.

[17] Carbone, *Originali o fotocopie*, 85, quoting *Positio*, 272.

[18] Salzano Acutis and Rodari, *Il segreto*, 185.

[19] Mohur, interview by author.

[20] Ylenia Spinelli, "Il mio amico Carlo Acutis, straordinario nella quotidianità", Chiesa di Milano (Archdiocese of Milan), October 4, 2020, https://www.chiesadimilano.it/news/chiesa-diocesi/il-mio-amico-carlo-acutis-straordinario-nella-quotidianita-336028.html.

[21] Sarah McBride, "Video Game Addiction, Now a Globally Recognized Illness, Seeks a Treatment", Bloomberg, February 23, 2022, https://bloomberg.com/news/articles/2022-02-23/video-game-addiction-recognized-by-world-health-organization.

[22] Will Conquer, *Carlo Acutis: A Millennial in Paradise* (Manchester, N.H.: Sophia Institute Press, 2021), 75.

[23] Twenge, *iGen*, 59.

[24] Carbone, *Originali o fotocopie*, 123, quoting *Positio*, 254.

[25] Carbone, *Originali o fotocopie*, 85, quoting *Positio*, 253–54.

7. In the Footsteps of Saint Francis

[1] William Stacchiotti, "Lo specialissimo rapporto di Carlo Acutis con san Francesco e la città di Assisi", *La Voce*, April 11, 2019, https://www.lavoce.it/rapporto-carlo-acutis-assisi/.

[2] "He soon eclipsed all the other saints of his age in popularity." Augustine Thompson, *Francis of Assisi: A New Biography* (Ithaca, N.Y.: Cornell University Press, 2012), 141.

[3] Courtney Mares, "Carlo Acutis Loved the Homeless, St. Francis of Assisi, and Souls in Purgatory", Catholic News Agency, October 7, 2020, https://catholicnewsagency.com/news/46124/carlo-acutis-loved-the-homeless-st-francis-of-assisi-and-souls-in-purgatory.

[4] Archbishop Domenico Sorrentino, *Originali, non fotocopie. Carlo Acutis e Francesco d'Assisi* (Perugia, Italy: Edizioni Francescane Italiane, 2019), 34.

[5] Ibid., 58.

[6] Ken Jennings, "This Italian Pine Forest Is Shaped Exactly Like . . . Italy", *Condé Nast Traveler*, October 1, 2018, https://cntraveler.com/story/this-italian-pine-forest-is-shaped-exactly-like-italy.

[7] Antonia Salzano Acutis and Paolo Rodari, *Il segreto di mio figlio. Perché Carlo Acutis è considerato un santo* (Milan: Piemme, 2021), 203.

[8] Ibid.

[9] Nicola Gori, *Eucaristia: La mia autostrada per il cielo. Biografia di Carlo Acutis (1991–2006)*, 8th ed. (Cinisello Balsamo [Milan]: San Paolo, 2007), 93.

[10] Antonia recalls that Carlo was about eight years old at the time. Salzano Acutis and Rodari, *Il segreto*, 174.

[11] Gori, *Eucaristia*, 93.

[12] "The Little Sisters of the Lamb", Community of the Lamb, https://communityofthelamb.org/little-sisters-of-the-lamb.

[13] Giorgio Maria Carbone, *Originali o fotocopie?* (Bologna: Edizioni Studio Domenicano, 2021), 171, quoting Congregatio de Causis Sanctorum, *Mediolanensis beatificationis et canonizationis servi Dei Carlo Acutis, Christifidelis laici (1991–2006): Positio super vita, virtutibus et fama sanctitatis* (Romae, 2017), 278 (hereafter cited as *Positio*).

[14] Carbone, *Originali o fotocopie*, 171, quoting *Positio*, 287.

[15] Carbone, *Originali o fotocopie*, 171.

[16] Carbone, *Originali o fotocopie*, 82.

[17] Carbone, *Originali o fotocopie*, 141, quoting *Positio*, 264.

[18] G.K. Chesterton, *Saint Thomas Aquinas and Saint Francis of Assisi* (San Francisco: Ignatius Press, 2002), 234.

[19] Sabrina Ferrisi, "Carlo Acutis 'Always Lived in the Presence of God'", *National Catholic Register*, June 27, 2020, https://ncregister.com/features/carlo-acutis-always-lived-in-the-presence-of-god.

[20] *Catechism of the Catholic Church* (CCC), no. 1471, quoting Paul VI, apostolic constitution *Indulgentiarum doctrina* (January 1, 1967), no. 1. The *Catechism* continues: "An indulgence is partial if it removes part of the temporal punishment due to sin, or plenary if it removes all punishment." *Indulgentiarum doctrina*, no. 2; cf. ibid., no. 3.

[21] Paul VI, apostolic constitution *Indulgentiarum doctrina*.

[22] For more information on the Porziuncola Indulgence, see Carl Bunderson, "On Aug. 2, You Can Get This St. Francis-Themed Indulgence", Catholic News Agency, August 2, 2020, https://catholicnewsagency.com/news/27816/on-aug-2-you-can-get-this-st-francis-themed-indulgence.

[23] Carbone, *Originali o fotocopie*, 147, quoting *Positio*, 271.

[24] Gori, *Eucaristia*, 118.

[25] Carbone, *Originali o fotocopie*, 147, quoting *Positio*, 271.

[26] Gori, *Eucaristia*, 118–19.

[27] Ibid., 120.

[28] Sorrentino, *Carlo Acutis e Francesco d'Assisi*, 13.

[29] Sorrentino, *Carlo Acutis e Francesco d'Assisi*, 13.

[30] Salzano Acutis and Rodari, *Il segreto*, 75.

8. Carlo on Pilgrimage: Eucharistic Miracles

[1] "What Is the Rimini Meeting?", Rimini Meeting, https://meetingrimini.org/en/il-meeting-e/che-cose-il-meeting/.

[2] "Carlo Acutis, quell'idea nata visitando il meeting", Rimini Meeting, 2020, https://www.meetingrimini.org/carlo-acutis-quellidea-nata-visitando-il-meeting/.

[3] *Piccolo catechismo eucaristico* panel: Antonia Acutis, Roberto Coggi, Antonio Gaspari, and Raffaello Vignali. A full transcript of the lecture presented at the August 20, 2002, Rimini Meeting has been published on the Rimini Meeting website: https://www.meetingrimini.org/wp-content/uploads/2002/08/1697_3_new-1.pdf.

[4] Giorgio Maria Carbone, *Originali o fotocopie?* (Bologna: Edizioni Studio Domenicano, 2021), 129.

[5] Roberto Coggi, *Piccolo catechismo eucaristico*, ed. Instituto San Clemente I, 4th ed. (Bologna, Italy: Edizioni Studio Domenicano, 2014), 30; Carbone, *Originali o fotocopie*, 129.

[6] Antonia Salzano Acutis and Paolo Rodari, *Il segreto di mio figlio. Perché Carlo Acutis è considerato un santo* (Milan: Piemme, 2021), 76–77. The fourth edition of *Piccolo catechismo eucaristico* does not include Carlo's graphics but instead has illustrations drawn by Sonia Maria Luce Possentini.

[7] "Catalogo", Mostre Meeting, https://www.meetingmostre.com/default.asp?id=344&text=&id_r=&start=2002#form.

[8] "International Exhibition Miracles of the Eucharist across the World, Devised and Planned by Carlo Acutis: Introductory Panel", Eucharistic Miracles of the World, http://www.miracolieucaristici.org/en/download/pannelloa.pdf.

[9] Ibid.

[10] According to the Dominican Publishing House, young Carlo Acutis collaborated in the creation of the eucharistic miracles book published at the same time as the exhibition by the San Clemente I Institute in 2005 "by collecting the images and photographs". Libreria Edizioni Studio Domenicano, *I miracoli eucaristici e le radici cristiane dell'Europa* (Bologna: Libreria Edizioni Studio Domenicano, 2021), https://www.edizionistudiodomenicano.it/prodotto/i-miracoli-eucaristici-e-le-radici-cristiane-delleuropa.

[11] Rajesh Mohur, interview by author, Milan, Italy, August 3, 2021.

[12] Ibid.

[13] Ibid.

[14] Joan Carroll Cruz, *Eucharistic Miracles* (Charlotte, N.C.: TAN Books, 2010), 51. (This book received an imprimatur in 1986 and was originally published in 1987.)

[15] "Eucharistic Miracle of Florence, Italy, 1230–1595", Eucharistic Miracles of the World, http://www.miracolieucaristici.org/en/liste/scheda.html?nat=italia&wh=firenze&ct=Florence,%201230-1595; Salzano Acutis and Rodari, *Il segreto*, 210.

[16] Ibid.

[17] Nicola Gori, *Eucaristia: La mia autostrada per il cielo. Biografia di Carlo Acutis (1991–2006)*, 8th ed. (Cinisello Balsamo [Milan]: San Paolo, 2007), 130; Salzano Acutis and Rodari, *Il segreto*, 197.

[18] Salzano Acutis and Rodari, *Il segreto*, 197.

[19] Gori, *Eucaristia*, 130.

[20] Video conference to Eucharistic Congress in Brazil. Text posted on Marcelo Tenorio, "Conferência de D. Antônia Acutis no congresso eucaristico", *Carlo Acutis, O Anjo da Juventude* (blog), May 23, 2013, http://carloacutisbr.blogspot.com/2013/05/conferencia-de-d-antonia-acutis-no.html.

[21] Franco Serafini, *A Cardiologist Examines Jesus: The Stunning Science behind Eucharistic Miracles* (Manchester, N.H.: Sophia Institute Press, 2021), 16.

[22] Cruz, *Eucharistic Miracles*, 3.

[23] Serafini, *A Cardiologist Examines Jesus*, 23.

[24] Serafini, *A Cardiologist Examines Jesus*, 24, citing Odoardo Linoli, "Ricerche istologiche, immunologiche e biochimiche sulla carne e sul sangue del miracolo eucaristico di Lanciano (VIII secolo)", *Quaderni sclavo di diagnostica* 7, no. 3 (September 1971).

[25] Zenit, "Physician Tells of Eucharistic Miracle of Lanciano", EWTN, May 5, 2005, https://ewtn.com/catholicism/library/physician-tells-of-eucharistic-miracle-of-lanciano-1866. For more details on the display of the eucharistic miracles exhibition, see "The Premiere of the Eucharistic Miracles Exhibition" in chapter 12.

[26] Ibid.

[27] "Gerona", International Exhibition Miracles of the Eucharist across the World, http://miracolieucaristici.org/en/liste/scheda.html?nat=spagna&wh=gerona&ct=Gerona,%201297.

[28] Salzano Acutis and Rodari, *Il segreto*, 91.

[29] Ibid.

[30] Tommaso da Celano, *Vita di Chiara d'Assisi*, ed. Giovanni Casoli (Rome: Città Nuova, 2020), 32–33.

[31] Carbone, *Originali o fotocopie*, 190; Salzano Acutis and Rodari, *Il segreto*, 109.

[32] Gori, *Eucaristia*, 133.

[33] "Third Apparition of the Angel", EWTN, https://ewtn.com/catholicism/devotions/third-apparition-of-the-angel-23359.

[34] Gori, *Eucaristia*, 87.

[35] Carbone, *Originali o fotocopie*, 190.

[36] Carbone, *Originali o fotocopie*, 135, quoting *Positio*, 537.

[37] Carbone, *Originali o fotocopie*, 190, quoting *Positio*, 537.

[38] Gori, *Eucaristia*, 132.

[39] Cruz, *Eucharistic Miracles*, 42.

[40] Salzano Acutis and Rodari, *Il segreto*, 216–17.

[41] Ibid., 74.

[42] "Alexandrina Maria Da Costa", Dicastero delle Cause dei Santi, http://causesanti.va/it/santi-e-beati/alexandrina-maria-da-costa.html.

[43] John Paul II, Homily for the Beatification of Six Servants of God (April 25, 2004).

[44] Salzano Acutis and Rodari, *Il segreto*, 74.

9. A Deepening Faith

[1] Michele Munno, *Quando le campane suonano a festa. La vita controcorrente del beato Carlo Acutis* (Camerata Picena, Italy: Shalom Editrice, 2002), 87.

[2] Giorgio Maria Carbone, *Originali o fotocopie?* (Bologna: Edizioni Studio Domenicano, 2021), 153–54, quoting Congregatio de Causis Sanctorum, *Mediolanensis beatificationis et canonizationis servi Dei Carlo Acutis, Christifidelis laici (1991–2006): Positio super vita, virtutibus et fama sanctitatis* (Romae, 2017), 362 (hereafter cited as *Positio*).

[3] Carbone, *Originali o fotocopie*, 153, quoting *Positio*, 202.

[4] Archbishop Domenico Sorrentino, *Originali, non fotocopie. Carlo Acutis e Francesco d'Assisi* (Perugia, Italy: Edizioni Francescane Italiane, 2019), 44, quoting *Positio*, 216–17.

[5] Will Conquer, *Carlo Acutis: A Millennial in Paradise* (Manchester, N.H.: Sophia Institute Press, 2021), 46–47; Antonia Salzano Acutis and Paolo Rodari, *Il segreto di mio figlio. Perché Carlo Acutis è considerato un santo* (Milan: Piemme, 2021), 190.

[6] Salzano Acutis and Rodari, *Il segreto*, 190.

[7] Ibid.

[8] Carbone, *Originali o fotocopie*, 141, quoting *Positio*, 271.

[9] Salzano Acutis and Rodari, *Il segreto*, 169.

[10] Ibid., 92.

[11] For more details, see the end of chapter 5 of this book.

[12] Carbone, *Originali o fotocopie*, 84.

[13] Salzano Acutis and Rodari, *Il segreto*, 170.

[14] Carbone, *Originali o fotocopie*, 86, quoting *Positio*, 147.

[15] Salzano Acutis and Rodari, *Il segreto*, 195.

[16] Ibid.

[17] Ibid., 196.

[18] Salzano Acutis and Rodari, *Il segreto*, 196.

[19] Rajesh Mohur, interview by author, Milan, Italy, August 3, 2021.

[20] *CCC* 1285.

[21] Testore had worked in the 1980s as the personal secretary of Cardinal Carlo Maria Marini, the archbishop of Milan from 1980 to 2004.

[22] *CCC* 1299.

[23] Nicola Gori, *Eucaristia: La mia autostrada per il cielo. Biografia di Carlo Acutis (1991–2006)*, 8th ed. (Cinisello Balsamo [Milan]: San Paolo, 2007), 83.

[24] Carbone, *Originali o fotocopie*, 101, quoting *Positio*, 353, 532.

[25] Carbone, *Originali o fotocopie*, 130, quoting *Positio*, 353.

[26] Carbone, *Originali o fotocopie*, 130, quoting *Positio*, 353.

[27] Carbone, *Originali o fotocopie*, 84.

[28] Compagnia di Maria Riparatrice, http://www.compagniamariariparatrice.it.

[29] Carbone, *Originali o fotocopie*, 135, quoting *Positio*, 192.

[30] Carbone, *Originali o fotocopie*, 136.

[31] Carbone, *Originali o fotocopie*, 136.

[32] Salzano Acutis and Rodari, *Il segreto*, 245; "The Servant of God Brother Ettore Boschini (1928–2004)," Ministers of the Infirm: Camillian Religious, March 8, 2016, https://www.camilliani.org/en/the-servant-of-god-brother-ettore-boschini-1928-2004/.

[33] Munno, *Quando le campane*, 168; Salzano Acutis and Rodari, *Il segreto*, 184.

[34] Munno, *Quando le campane*, 104.

10. Heroic Virtue Online

[1] "Papal Transition 2005 Web Archive", Library of Congress Web Archives, https://www.loc.gov/collections/papal-transition-2005-web-archive/about-this-collection/.

[2] Chris Wilson, "Jesus of Wikipedia", *Slate*, January 14, 2011, https://slate.com/technology/2011/01/wikipedia-s-10th-birthday-and-what-jesus-page-can-tell-us-about-it.html; "Jesus: En.wikipedia.org", General Statistics, XTools, https://xtools.wmflabs.org/articleinfo/en.wikipedia.org/Jesus.

[3] Kenneth Muenstermann, "A German Pope," *Historic Christianity* (blog), April 21, 2005, archived at https://webarchive.loc.gov/all/20050502063306/http://historic-christianity.blogspot.com/. The word "blog" is a shortened form of "weblog". The term describes the format of such sites, which usually consists of a series of dated entries, similar to what is found in a journal.

[4] "Papal Transition 2005 Web Archive".

[5] "Dennis for Pope", 2005, Library of Congress Web Archive, https://www.loc.gov/item/lcwaN0008110/.

[6] Father Roberto Gazzaniga (Carlo's high school chaplain), telephone interview by author, December 1, 2021.

[7] Mary Farrow, "What Is Acedia, How Do You Pronounce It, and Why Does This Priest Tweet about It?", Catholic News Agency, May 19, 2020, https://catholicnewsagency.com/news/44564/what-is-acedia-how-do-you-pronounce-it-and-why-does-this-priest-tweet-about-it.

[8] Giorgio Maria Carbone, *Originali o fotocopie?* (Bologna: Edizioni Studio Domenicano, 2021), 39, quoting Congregatio de Causis Sanctorum, *Mediolanensis beatificationis et canonizationis servi Dei Carlo Acutis, Christifidelis laici (1991–2006): Positio super vita, virtutibus et fama sanctitatis* (Romae, 2017), 303 (hereafter cited as *Positio*).

[9] *CCC* 1324–27, quoting *LG* 11.

[10] Dicastero delle Cause dei Santi (Dicastery for the Causes of Saints), Decree on the Virtues of Servant of God Carlo Acutis (July 5, 2018), http://www.causesanti.va/it/santi-e-beati/carlo-acutis.html.

[11] Francesco Occhetta, *Carlo Acutis beato. La vita oltre il confine* (Gorle, Italy: Editrice Velar, 2013).

[12] Antonia Salzano Acutis and Paolo Rodari, *Il segreto di mio figlio. Perché Carlo Acutis è considerato un santo* (Milan: Piemme, 2021), 187.

[13] Nicola Gori, *Eucaristia: La mia autostrada per il cielo. Biografia di Carlo Acutis (1991–2006)*, 8th ed. (Cinisello Balsamo [Milan]: San Paolo, 2007), 57.

[14] Carbone, *Originali o fotocopie*, 114, quoting *Positio*, 315.

[15] Synod of Bishops, 11th Ordinary General Assembly, *Instrumentum laboris* (2005).

[16] Salzano Acutis and Rodari, *Il segreto*, 79.

[17] Amato, *Decreto sulle virtù.*

[18] Carbone, *Originali o fotocopie*, 95, quoting *Positio*, 314.

[19] Carbone, *Originali o fotocopie*, 35, quoting *Positio*, 291, 324.

[20] Carbone, *Originali o fotocopie*, quoting *Positio*, 291.

[21] Carbone, *Originali o fotocopie*, 159, quoting *Positio*, 303, 324.

[22] John Mark Haney, "Teenagers and Pornography Addiction: Treating the Silent Epidemic", *Vistas Online* (American Counseling Association), 2006, https://www.counseling.org/docs/default-source/vistas/teenagers-and-pornography-addiction-treating-the-silent-epidemic.pdf?sfvrsn=3ddd7e2c_10.

[23] Janice Wolak, Kimberly Mitchell, and David Finkelhor, "Unwanted and Wanted Exposure to Online Pornography in a National Sample of Youth Internet Users", *Pediatrics* 119, no. 2 (February 2007): 247–57.

[24] Carbone, *Originali o fotocopie*, 179, quoting *Positio*, 312.

[25] Bree Dail, "Mother of Soon-to-Be Blessed Carlo Acutis: 'Jesus Was His First Priority'", *National Catholic Register*, February 27, 2020,

https://ncregister.com/interview/mother-of-soon-to-be-blessed-carlo-acutis-jesus-was-his-first-priority; See also Salzano Acutis and Rodari, *Il segreto*, 186.

[26] Carbone, *Originali o fotocopie*, 177–78, quoting *Positio*, 137.

[27] Carbone, *Originali o fotocopie*, 175, quoting *Positio*, 126.

[28] Archbishop Domenico Sorrentino, *Originali, non fotocopie. Carlo Acutis e Francesco d'Assisi* (Perugia, Italy: Edizioni Francescane Italiane, 2019), 44, quoting *Positio*, 312.

[29] Carbone, *Originali o fotocopie,* 175, quoting *Positio*, 241.

[30] Carbone, *Originali o fotocopie*, 63, quoting *Positio*, 291.

[31] Carbone, *Originali o fotocopie*, 177, quoting *Positio*, 311. The reference is to 1 Corinthians 6:19.

11. Carlo's Confessors

[1] Antonia Salzano Acutis and Paolo Rodari, *Il segreto di mio figlio. Perché Carlo Acutis è considerato un santo* (Milan: Piemme, 2021), 114.

[2] Salzano Acutis and Rodari, *Il Segreto*, 115.

[3] Ibid., 114.

[4] "Intervista alla madre di Carlo Acutis", Mondocrea, February 7, 2017, https://www.mondocrea.it/carlo-acutis-un-adolescente-modello-per-i-giovani-doggi/.

[5] Nicola Gori, *Eucaristia: La mia autostrada per il cielo. Biografia di Carlo Acutis (1991–2006)*, 8th ed. (Cinisello Balsamo [Milan]: San Paolo, 2007), 98.

[6] See the Porziuncola section in chapter 7.

[7] Giorgio Maria Carbone, *Originali o fotocopie?* (Bologna: Edizioni Studio Domenicano, 2021), 148, quoting Congregatio de Causis Sanctorum, *Mediolanensis beatificationis et canonizationis servi Dei Carlo Acutis, Christifidelis laici (1991–2006): Positio super vita, virtutibus et fama sanctitatis* (Romae, 2017), 373 (hereafter cited as *Positio*).

[8] Dodici Porte, "Lutto", YouTube video, 0:40, November 19, 2010, https://youtu.be/9pSMnFEDOsc.

[9] Gori, *Eucaristia*, 87.

[10] Carbone, *Originali o fotocopie*, 128, quoting *Positio*, 372.

[11] Gori, *Eucaristia*, 87.

[12] Carbone, *Originali o fotocopie*, 176, quoting *Positio*, 371.

[13] Carbone, *Originali o fotocopie*, 96 and 188, quoting *Positio*, 371.

[14] Carbone, *Originali o fotocopie*, 42, quoting *Positio*, 371.

[15] Will Conquer, *Carlo Acutis: A Millennial in Paradise* (Manchester, N.H.: Sophia Institute Press, 2021), 70–71.

[16] Carbone, *Originali o fotocopie*, 124, quoting *Positio*, 520.

[17] "Intervista alla madre di Carlo Acutis".

[18] Carbone, *Originali o fotocopie*, 123, quoting *Positio*, 254.

[19] Carbone, *Originali o fotocopie*, 126, quoting *Positio*, 322.

[20] Carbone, *Originali o fotocopie*, 123, quoting *Positio*, 229.

[21] *I Am with You: A Documentary on Carlo Acutis*, a Cristiana video and EWTN production, 2021, 35:01, https://ondemand.ewtn.com/free/Home/Play/381-373197.

[22] Ibid.

12. High School Holiness

[1] "Pope Leo's Jubilee", *Catholic Telegraph*, March 9, 1893, https://thecatholicnewsarchive.org/?a=d&d=TCT18930309-01.2.17&e=-------en-20--1--txt-txIN.

[2] "Manifesto-Il sogno di tutte le private: la perfetta 'scuola per ricchi'", Federazione Lavoratori della Conoscenza, October 14, 2003, https://www.flcgil.it/rassegna-stampa/nazionale/manifesto-il-sogno-di-tutte-le-private-la-perfetta-scuola-per-ricchi.flc.

[3] Nicola Gori, *Eucaristia: La mia autostrada per il cielo. Biografia di Carlo Acutis (1991–2006)*, 8th ed. (Cinisello Balsamo [Milan]: San Paolo, 2007), 56.

[4] Ibid., 45–46.

[5] Father Roberto Gazzaniga, telephone interview by author, December 1, 2021.

[6] Ibid.

[7] Giorgio Maria Carbone, *Originali o fotocopie?* (Bologna: Edizioni Studio Domenicano, 2021), 163, quoting Congregatio de Causis Sanctorum, *Mediolanensis beatificationis et canonizationis servi Dei Carlo Acutis, Christifidelis laici (1991–2006): Positio super vita, virtutibus et fama sanctitatis* (Romae, 2017), 144 (hereafter cited as *Positio*).

[8] Andrea Galli, "10 Anni fa moriva il 15enne Carlo Acutis la purezza della fede e la fama di santità", *Avvenire*, October 12, 2016, https://avvenire.it/chiesa/pagine/carlo-acutis-la-purezza-della-fede-3.

[9] Ibid.

[10] Nicola Gori, the postulator of Carlo's cause for beatification, collected many of the testimonies from Carlo's classmates from high school and published them anonymously in his book, *Eucaristia: La mia autostrada per il cielo*.

[11] Annamaria Braccini, "Normalità, entusiasmo, testimonianza: ecco la santità di Carlo Acutis", Chiesa di Milano (Archdiocese of Milan), October 4, 2020, https://www.chiesadimilano.it/news/chiesa-diocesi/normalita-entusiasmo-testimonianza-ecco-la-santita-di-carlo-acutis-336235.html.

[12] Gori, *Eucaristia*, 45.

[13] Ibid., 55.

[14] Gazzaniga, interview by author.

[15] Antonia Salzano Acutis and Paolo Rodari, *Il segreto di mio figlio. Perché Carlo Acutis è considerato un santo* (Milan: Piemme, 2021), 76.

[16] Gazzaniga, interview by author.

[17] Gazzaniga, interview by author.

[18] Gori, *Eucaristia*, 55.

[19] Carbone, *Originali o fotocopie*, 184, quoting *Positio*, 390.

[20] Gori, *Eucaristia*, 46.

[21] Ibid., 44–45.

[22] Carbone, *Originali o fotocopie*, 185, quoting *Positio*, 163.

[23] Salzano Acutis and Rodari, *Il segreto*, 171.

[24] Carbone, *Originali o fotocopie*, 166, quoting *Positio*, 305, 438.

[25] Carbone, *Originali o fotocopie*, 24, quoting *Positio*, 305.

[26] Ibid.

[27] Salzano Acutis and Rodari, *Il segreto*, 74.

[28] Archbishop Domenico Sorrentino, *Originali, non fotocopie. Carlo Acutis e Francesco d'Assisi* (Perugia, Italy: Edizioni Francescane Italiane, 2019), 44, quoting *Positio*, 305.

[29] Salzano Acutis and Rodari, *Il segreto*, 73.

[30] Gori, *Eucaristia*, 45–46.

[31] Salzano Acutis and Rodari, *Il segreto*, 167.

[32] Ibid., 168.

[33] Sorrentino, *Carlo Acutis e Francesco d'Assisi*, 37, quoting Salzano's testimony in *Positio*, 308.

[34] Courtney Mares, "Carlo Acutis' Love for the Homeless Remembered by Friends ahead of Beatification", Catholic News Agency, October 7, 2020, https://catholicnewsagency.com/news/46124/carlo-acutis-loved-the-homeless-st-francis-of-assisi-and-souls-in-purgatory.

[35] Ibid.

[36] Ibid.

[37] Carbone, *Originali o Fotocopie*, 161, quoting *Positio*, 268.

[38] Stefano Lorenzetto, "Antonia Salzano: 'Il miracolo di Carlo Acutis, mio figlio, morto 15enne di leucemia: Un santo per il web'", *Corriere della Sera*, September 4, 2020, https://tinyurl.com/2p9bwn9p.

[39] Carbone, *Originali o fotocopie*, 162, quoting *Positio*, 173.

[40] *I Am with You: A Documentary on Carlo Acutis*, a Cristiana video and EWTN production, 2021, 35:01, https://ondemand.ewtn.com/free/Home/Play/381-373197.

[41] "Ampia rassegna fotografica sui Miracoli Eucaristici in una mostra a Roma", Zenit, May 19, 2005, https://it.zenit.org/2005/05/19/ampia-rassegna-fotografica-sui-miracoli-eucaristici-in-una-mostra-a-roma/.

[42] "Quando l'ostia consacrata diventa carne e sangue: le risposte della Scienza e della Fede. Un congresso, a Roma, sui Miracoli Eucaristici", *Agenzia Fides*, April 29, 2005, http://fides.org/it/news/6251-Quando_l_ostia_consacrata_diventa_carne_e_sangue_le_risposte_della_Scienza_e_della_Fede_Un_congresso_a_Roma_sui_Miracoli_Eucaristici.

[43] Monsignor Raffaello Martinelli said in an interview in 2005 that the display panels were offered thanks to "the kind willingness of Antonia Salzano Acutis". "Exhibition Focuses on Eucharistic Miracles: Interview with a Promoter, Monsignor Raffaello Martinelli", Zenit, October 17, 2005, https://zenit.org/2005/10/17/exhibition-focuses-on-eucharistic-miracles/.

[44] Carbone, *Originali o fotocopie*, 11.

[45] Carbone, *Originali o fotocopie*, 11–12.

[46] Ibid., 12.

[47] Ibid., 22, quoting *Positio*, 292.

[48] Edward Young, *Conjectures on Original Composition* (1759), no. 164, https://rpo.library.utoronto.ca/content/conjectures-original-composition-1759. Note that Christian author John Mason also published a book in 1993 with the title *You're Born an Original, Don't Die a Copy!*

[49] Carbone, *Originali o fotocopie*, 23.

[50] C. S. Lewis, *Mere Christianity* (New York: HarperCollins, 2001), 226.

[51] Carbone, *Originali o fotocopie*, 22.

[52] Ibid., 112, quoting *Positio*, 316.

[53] Carbone, *Originali o fotocopie*, 40.

[54] Carbone, *Originali o fotocopie*, 40, quoting *Positio*, 137.

[55] Carbone, *Originali o fotocopie*, 182, quoting *Positio*, 175.

[56] Carbone, *Originali o fotocopie*, 180, quoting *Positio*, 204.

[57] Carbone, *Originali o fotocopie*, 178, quoting *Positio*, 390.

[58] Gori, *Eucaristia*, 45–46.

[59] Carbone, *Originali o fotocopie*, 178–79, quoting *Positio*, 311.

[60] Salzano Acutis and Rodari, *Il segreto*, 181.

[61] Ibid., 58.

[62] Ibid., 55.

[63] Ibid.

[64] Ibid., 68–69.

[65] Ibid.

[66] Ibid., 69.

[67] Carbone, *Originali o fotocopie*, 135, quoting *Positio*, 316.

[68] Salzano Acutis and Rodari, *Il segreto*, 53.

[69] Ibid., 53–54.

[70] Ibid., 54.

[71] Ibid., 53.

[72] Carbone, *Originali o fotocopie*, 202.

[73] "Santuario S. Antonio M. Zaccaria", Istituto Zaccaria, https://istitutozaccaria.it/it/strutture-servizi/santuario-s-antonio-m-zaccaria.

13. "I Offer My Suffering"

[1] Antonia Salzano Acutis and Paolo Rodari, *Il segreto di mio figlio. Perché Carlo Acutis è considerato un santo* (Milan: Piemme, 2021), 11.

[2] Teena and Aditya Ayyagari, "Talk to Rajesh Mohur about Blessed Carlo Acutis", YouTube video, 1:30:35, November 13, 2020, https://youtu.be/WxQ6MAwqIPQ.

[3] Rajesh testified to the Vatican that he remembers that Carlo said, "All that I am suffering I offer to the Lord." Giorgio Maria Carbone, *Originali o Fotocopie?* (Bologna: Edizioni Studio Domenicano, 2021), 203, quoting Congregatio de Causis Sanctorum, *Mediolanensis beatificationis et canonizationis servi Dei Carlo Acutis, Christifidelis laici (1991–2006): Positio super vita, virtutibus et fama sanctitatis* (Romae, 2017), 167 (hereafter cited as *Positio*).

[4] "Carlo Acutis: Biografia", Dicastero delle Cause dei Santi, http://causesanti.va/it/santi-e-beati/carlo-acutis.html. Carlo's grandmother Luana testified to the Vatican that she remembered Carlo's words as: "I offer my life for the pope, for the Church, in order not to go through purgatory and to go straight to heaven", according to Carbone, *Originali o Fotocopie*, 203, quoting *Positio*, 269, 278. See also Salzano Acutis and Rodari, *Il segreto*, 11.

[5] *Catechism of the Catholic Church* (*CCC*), no. 1505.

[6] Salzano Acutis and Rodari, *Il segreto*, 13.

[7] "La parotite".

[8] Stefano Lorenzetto, "Antonia Salzano: 'Il miracolo di Carlo Acutis, mio figlio, morto 15enne di leucemia: Un santo per il web'", *Corriere della Sera*, September 4, 2020, https://tinyurl.com/2p9bwn9p.

[9] Salzano Acutis and Rodari, *Il segreto*, 14.

[10] Ibid., 16.

[11] Carbone, *Originali o fotocopie*, 61, quoting *Positio*, 313.

[12] Carbone, *Originali o fotocopie*, 197, quoting *Positio*, 270, 284, 324.

[13] Salzano Acutis and Rodari, *Il segreto*, 16.

[14] Nicola Gori, *Eucaristia: La mia autostrada per il cielo. Biografia di Carlo Acutis (1991–2006)*, 8th ed. (Cinisello Balsamo [Milan]: San Paolo, 2007), 106.

[15] Ibid.

[16] Carbone, *Originali o fotocopie*, 201, quoting *Positio*, 173.

[17] Andrea Biondi and Mòmcilo Jankovic, "Lettera dei Medici Andrea-Biondi e Mòmcilo Jankovic della clinica pediatrica e Centro di Ematologia Pediatrica Allospedale San Gerardo di Monza", Diocesi di Assisi (Diocese of Assisi), http://www.diocesiassisi.it/wp-content/uploads/sites/2/2020/10/13/Lettera-dei-medici-Andrea-Biondi-e-Momcilo-Jankovic-della-Clinica-pediatrica-e-Centro-di-ematologia-pediatrica-allospedale-San-Gerardo-di-Monza.pdf; Courtney Mares, "Blessed Carlo Acutis' Doctors Recall His Last Days in Hospital", Catholic News Agency, October 16, 2020, https://catholicnewsagency.com/news/46238/blessed-carlo-acutis-doctors-recall-his-last-days-in-hospital.

[18] Salzano Acutis and Rodari, *Il segreto*, 165–66.

[19] Carbone, *Originali o fotocopie*, 207, quoting *Positio*, 290.

[20] Carbone, *Originali o fotocopie*, 199, quoting *Positio*, 289.

[21] Mares, "Doctors Recall His Last Days in Hospital".

[22] "Reflection of Cardinal Justin Rigali on the Mystery of Christian Death", Catholic Preaching, November 19, 2013, http://www.catholicpreaching.com/wp/wp-content/uploads/2013/11/Cardinal-Rigali-on-Priests-Preparing-for-Death.pdf.

[23] Lorenzetto, "Antonia Salzano: Il miracolo di Carlo Acutis".

[24] Milena Castigli, "Carlo Acutis l'influencer di Dio", *In Terris*, August 18, 2021, https://www.interris.it/copertina/carlo-acutis-influencer-dio/?fbclid=IwAR07noiaeTPG3n5iha9VGPuzcTQFDTFtnAJYe-By_k63d96x19KfGClrlo4.

[25] Salzano Acutis and Rodari, *Il segreto*, 26.

[26] Ibid., 44–45.

[27] "E un altro saluto . . . Nel silenzio traffigente del congedo di un giovane amico", *Il Segno*, November 11, 2006, A, archived at http://www.carloacutis.com/img/association/articles/pdf/36.pdf.

[28] Ibid.

[29] Salzano Acutis and Rodari, *Il segreto*, 45–46.

[30] Ibid.

[31] Ibid.

[32] Obituary for Carlo Acutis, *Corriere della Sera*, October 14, 2006, 54, archived at http://carloacutis.com/img/association/articles/pdf/119.pdf; Obituary for Carlo Acutis, *La Stampa*, October 14, 2006, http://carloacutis.com/img/association/articles/pdf/126.pdf.

[33] Salzano Acutis and Rodari, *Il segreto*, 49.

[34] Gazzaniga, interview by author.

[35] Gori, *Eucaristia*, 56.

[36] David Ramos, "Mexican Bishop: Apparent Eucharistic Miracle of Tixtla Has Yet to Be Approved by Rome", Catholic News Agency, February 16, 2022, https://www.catholicnewsagency.com/news/250409/mexican-bishop-apparent-eucharistic-miracle-of-tixtla-has-yet-to-be-approved-by-rome.

[37] Salzano Acutis and Rodari, *Il segreto*, 293.

[38] Carbone, *Originali o fotocopie*, 194, quoting *Positio*, 323.

[39] Carbone, *Originali o fotocopie*, 194.

[40] Carbone, *Originali o fotocopie*, quoting *Positio*, 323.

[41] Carbone, *Originali o fotocopie*, 195, quoting *Positio*, 269.

[42] Fabio Negri, "Carlo, esempio per tanti giovani", http://carloacutis.com/img/association/articles/pdf/6.pdf.

[43] "Italy Moved by Teen Who Offers Life for the Church and the Pope", Catholic News Agency, October 24, 2007, https://catholicnewsagency.com/news/10773/italy-moved-by-teen-who-offers-life-for-the-church-and-the-pope.

[44] According to the Dominican publishing house that published some of the books by the San Clemente Institute, the institute was later absorbed into the Friends of Carlo Acutis Association. "Istituto San Clemente", Libreria Edizioni Studio Domenicano, https://edizionistudiodomenicano.it/autori/istituto-san-clemente/.

[45] The domain of www.carloacutis.com was registered in Italy on May 24, 2007. "Registration Data Lookup Tool: carloacutis.com", ICANN Lookup, last visited January 9, 2023, https://lookup.icann.org/en/lookup.

[46] "Contatti", Friends of Carlo Acutis Association.

[47] "Beato Carlo Acutis", Gruppo Ufficiale dell'Associazione Amici di Carlo Acutis, Facebook, December 3, 2008, https://www.facebook.com/groups/CarloAcutis/about.

[48] "Testimonianze", CarloAcutis.com, May 19, 2009, archived at https://web.archive.org/web/20090519030941/http://www.carloacutis.com/pages/testimonianze.html, accessed via Internet Archive.

[49] The homepage of the eucharistic miracles website on September 19, 2008, stated that the exhibition comprised 142 laminated panels

and had visited more than 500 parishes in Italy and in other countries. At this time, the website had already been translated into other languages, with pages in Spanish and French. "Los Milagros Eucarísticos en el Mundo", Eucharistic Miracles of the World, September 19, 2008, archived at https://web.archive.org/web/20080919214855/http://www.miracolieucaristici.org/addLanguage/espanol.html.

[50] According to the Internet Corporation for Assigned Names and Numbers (ICANN)—the organization responsible for Internet Protocol (IP) addresses and domain-name system management—and the WHOIS data tool, developed by the Internet Engineering Task Force, the domain of www.miracolieucaristici.org was registered by Antonia Salzano in Italy on November 29, 2007. "Registration Data Lookup Tool: www.miracolieucaristici.org," ICANN Lookup, https://lookup.icann.org/en/lookup; "Domain Information: Miracolieucaristici.org", WHOIS, https://whois.com/whois/miracolieucaristici.org.

[51] The earliest record of the webpage in the Internet Archive WayBack Machine is September 19, 2008. "Los Milagros Eucarísticos en el Mundo", "Eucharistic Miracles of the World", September 19, 2008, archived at https://web.archive.org/web/20080919214855/http://www.miracolieucaristici.org/addLanguage/espanol.html.

[52] Marcelo Tenorio, "Caríssimos divulgadores de Carlo Acutis", *Carlo Acutis, O Anjo Da Juventude* (blog), November 4, 2012, http://carloacutisbr.blogspot.com/2012/11/mensagem-aos-divulgadores-de-carlo.html.

14. A Miracle in Brazil

[1] "Nostra Signora di Aparecida", Vatican News, https://vaticannews.va/it/santo-del-giorno/10/12/nostra-signora-di-aparecida.html.

[2] Marcélo Tenorio, "Caríssimos divulgadores de Carlo Acutis", *Carlo Acutis, O Anjo Da Juventude* (blog), November 4, 2012, http://carloacutisbr.blogspot.com/2012/11/mensagem-aos-divulgadores-de-carlo.html.

[3] "Il miracolo", Dicastero della Cause dei Santi (Dicastery for the Causes of Saints), http://www.causesanti.va/it/santi-e-beati/carlo-acutis.html; Agência Estado, "Família de Campo Grande celebra beatificação de Carlo Acutis", *Correio Braziliense*, October 3, 2020,

https://correiobraziliense.com.br/brasil/2020/10/4879805-familia-de-campo-grande-celebra-beatificacao-de-carlo-acutis.html.

[4] "Il miracolo".

[5] Filipe Domingues, "Carlo Acutis Could Become the First Millennial Saint. Here's the Story behind His First Miracle", *America*, November 20, 2020, https://www.americamagazine.org/faith/2020/11/20/blessed-carlo-acutis-saint-relics-millennial-miracle.

[6] Agência Estado, "Família de Campo Grande".

[7] Domingues, "Carlo Acutis Could Become the First Millennial Saint".

[8] Ibid.

[9] "The recovery of the child took place during the Holy Mass, immediately after the kissing of the relic." See "Il miracolo".

[10] Lucia Morel "'Ciberapóstolo' será beatificado dia 11 após milagre comprovado em Campo Grande", *Campo Grande News*, October 2, 2020, https://campograndenews.com.br/cidades/capital/ciberapostolo-sera-beatificado-dia-11-apos-milagre-comprovado-em-campo-grande.

[11] Domingues, "Carlo Acutis Could Become the First Millennial Saint".

[12] Ibid.

[13] Ibid.

[14] Robert J. Sarno, "Steps to Sainthood", Solanus Casey Center, https://solanuscasey.org/about-blessed-solanus-casey/road-to-sainthood.

[15] *Catechism of the Catholic Church* (*CCC*), no. 824, quoting *SC* 10.

[16] *CCC* 828, quoting *CL* 16, 3.

[17] Sarno, "Steps to Sainthood".

[18] Facebook had existed before 2006, but it was limited to college students. Note that Myspace's popularity peaked around 2006.

[19] Andrew Perrin, "Social Media Usage: 2005–2015", Pew Research Center, October 8, 2015, https://pewresearch.org/internet/2015/10/08/social-networking-usage-2005-2015/.

[20] "I passi del cammino verso la santita", Dicastero della Cause dei Santi (Dicastery for the Causes of Saints), http://www.causesanti.va/it/i-passi-del-cammino-verso-la-santita/approfondimenti.html#fama-di-santit%C3%A0.

[21] Carbone, *Originali o fotocopie*, 15.

[22] An excerpt of the documentary, *My Highway to Heaven: Carlo Acutis and the Eucharist*, was played at the event, which was held in the Vatican City State's film library on October 26, 2016.

"Carlo Acutis: Don Costa (Lev), 'Rilancia dei valori che in lui diventano più attuali e moderni'", Società per l'Informazione Religiosa (SIR), October 26, 2016, https://www.agensir.it/quotidiano/2016/10/26/carlo-acutis-don-costa-lev-rilancia-dei-valori-che-in-lui-diventano-piu-attuali-e-moderni/. Both Carlo's former parish priest, Monsignor Gianfranco Poma, and Carlo's mother spoke at the press conference.

[23] Rossi, "Carlo, genio del computer morto a 15 anni".

[24] Ibid.

[25] Annamaria Braccini, "Scola: 'Carlo Acutis è un dono grande per la nostra conversione'", Chiesa di Milano (Archdiocese of Milan), November 24, 2016, https://www.chiesadimilano.it/news/chiesa-diocesi/scola-carlo-acutis-e-un-dono-grande-per-la-nostra-conversione-92951.html.

[26] Courtney Mares, "'Holy Mayor' Giorgio La Pira Takes Next Step to Sainthood", Catholic News Agency, July 5, 2018, https://catholicnewsagency.com/news/38804/holy-mayor-giorgio-la-pira-takes-next-step-to-sainthood. Carlo's body was also exhumed during this stage on June 23, 2018.

[27] "Carlo Acutis", Vatican Dicastery for the Causes of Saints, accessed May 25, 2024, archived at https://web.archive.org/web/20240525122403/https://www.causesanti.va/it/santi-e-beati/carlo-acutis.html.

15. Carlo Goes Viral

[1] "Coronavirus Disease 2019 (COVID-19) Situation Report—33", World Health Organization, February 22, 2020, https://who.int/publications/m/item/situation-report---33.

[2] "Coronavirus. Chiese aperte ma Messe sospese. La preghiera dell'arcivescovo Delpini", *Avvenire*, February 24, 2020, https://www.avvenire.it/chiesa/pagine/milano-l-arcivescovo-delpini-un-pensiero-di-benedizione.

[3] AFP, "In Bergamo, Memory of Coffin-Filled Trucks Still Haunts", France 24, March 18, 2021, https://www.france24.com/en/live-news/20210318-in-bergamo-memory-of-coffin-filled-trucks-still-haunts.

[4] Carlo's mother told one journalist that she had had a dream after Carlo died in which Carlo told her that she would be a mother again. See Laura Badaracchi, "Mio figlio mi disse in sogno: 'Sarai di nuovo mamma'", *Famiglia Cristiana*, October 1, 2020, https://www.famiglia cristiana.it/articolo/antonia-salzano-acutis-la-mamma-di-carlo-acutis -mio-figlio-mi-disse-in-sogno-sarai-di-nuovo-mamma.aspx.

[5] Courtney Mares, "Beatification of Carlo Acutis: The First Millennial to Be Declared Blessed", Catholic News Agency, October 10, 2020, https://catholicnewsagency.com/news/46167/beatification-of-carlo-acutis-the-first-millennial-to-be-declared-blessed.

[6] Ibid.

[7] Ibid.

[8] Google search data for "eucharistic miracles" in 2020, Google Trends, https://trends.google.com/trends/explore?date=2020-01-01% 202020-12-31&q=Eucharistic%20miracles.

[9] Pope Francis, Angelus, October 11, 2020.

[10] "Chiusa la tomba di Carlo Acutis, sara'riaperta definitivamente dopo l'emergenza pandemica", Sanctuario della Spogliazione Assisi, October 20, 2020, https://www.assisisantuariospogliazione.it/2020/10 /20/chiusa-la-tomba-di-carlo-acutis-sara-riaperta-definitivamente-dopo -lemergenza-pandemica/.

[11] Pope Francis, Letter to the Bishop of Assisi for the Inauguration of the Santuario della Spogliazione (April 16, 2017), https://press.vatic an.va/content/salastampa/it/bollettino/pubblico/2017/04/16/0245/00 557.html.

[12] Philip Kosloski, "What Does the IHS Monogram Mean?" Aleteia, May 15, 2017, https://aleteia.org/2017/05/15/what-does-the-ihs-mono gram-mean.

[13] The display was designed by Alfio Barabani based on illustrations by Mario Cossu."Ideazione e progetto della tomba", CarloA cutis.com, http://carloacutis.com/it/association/ideazione-e-progetto -della-tomba "Le formelle disegnate da Mario Cossu nella tomba del beato Carlo Acutis", Beato Carlo Acutis (Friends of Carlo Acutis Association), Facebook, December 11, 2020, https://www.facebook.com

/beatocarloacutisufficiale/posts/-esclusivo-le-formelle-disegnate-da-ma rio-cossu-nella-tomba-del-beato-carlo-acut/1114148422375139/.

[14] John 13:23. See Beato Carlo Acutis (Friends of Carlo Acutis Association), Facebook, December 11, 2020, https://www.facebook.com /beatocarloacutisufficiale/photos/pcb.1114148422375139/1114122119 044436.

[15] "Ideazione e progetto della tomba"; "Le Formelle disegnate da Mario Cossu nella tomba Del Beato Carlo Acutis".

[16] Courtney Mares, "Tomb of Carlo Acutis Is Opened for Veneration Ahead of Beatification", Catholic News Agency, October 1, 2020, https://catholicnewsagency.com/news/46045/tomb-of-carlo -acutis-is-opened-for-veneration-ahead-of-beatification.

[17] Courtney Mares, "Public Veneration of Blessed Carlo Acutis' Tomb Extended as Pilgrims Flock to Assisi", Catholic News Agency, October 14, 2020, https://catholicnewsagency.com/news/46211/pub lic-veneration-of-blessed-carlo-acutis-tomb-extended-as-pilgrims-flock -to-assisi.

[18] Melissa Guerrero, "How Losing My Eyesight—and Blessed Carlo Acutis's Intercession—Saved My Life", EpicPew, February 25, 2021, https://epicpew.com/how-losing-my-eyesight-and-blessed-carlo -acutiss-intercession-saved-my-life/.

[19] Ibid.

16. What Carlo Can Teach Gen Z

[1] Pope Francis, postsynodal apostolic exhortation *Christus vivit* (March 25, 2019), no. 104.

[2] Ibid., nos. 104–7.

[3] *Catechism of the Catholic Church* (*CCC*) 1084.

[4] Jean M. Twenge, *iGen* (New York: Atria Books, 2017), 2.

[5] Ibid.

[6] "Fall 2022 Survey: Taking Stock with Teens", Piper Sandler, October 11, 2022, https://www.pipersandler.com/1col.aspx?id=6216.

[7] Twenge, *iGen*, 2.

[8] Jason M. Nagata et al., "Screen Time Use among US Adolescents during the COVID-19 Pandemic", *JAMA Pediatrics* 176, no. 1 (January 2022): 94, https://doi.org/10.1001/jamapediatrics.2021.4334.

[9] Twenge, *iGen*, 56, citing Nancy Jo Sales, *American Girls: Social Media and the Secret Lives of Teenagers* (New York: Vintage Books, 2016).

[10] Pope Francis, Lenten Message (February 24, 2022).

[11] Twenge, *iGen*, 3–4.

[12] Sally C. Curtin, "State Suicide Rates among Adolescents and Young Adults Aged 10–24: United States, 2000–2018", *National Vital Statistics Reports* 69, no. 11 (September 11, 2020), CDC, https://cdc.gov/nchs/data/nvsr/nvsr69/NVSR-69-11-508.pdf.

[13] Twenge, *iGen*, 82.

[14] Ibid., 83–84.

[15] Neil Postman, *Amusing Ourselves to Death* (New York: Penguin Books, 2006).

[16] Statistics from eighth graders during the years 2013–2015. Twenge, *iGen*, 78.

[17] Courtney Mares, "Pope Francis' Lenten Message: Addiction to Digital Media Can Hurt Human Relationships", Catholic News Agency, February 24, 2022, https://catholicnewsagency.com/news/250467/pope-francis-lent-2022-message-addiction-to-digital-media-can-hurt-human-relationships.

[18] Twenge, *iGen*, 121.

[19] Ibid., 126.

[20] Ibid., 120.

[21] Ibid., 93.

[22] Christine Rousselle, "Millennial and Gen Z Catholics Love Carlo Acutis. Here's Why", Catholic News Agency, October 12, 2021, https://catholicnewsagency.com/news/46147/millennial-and-gen-z-catholics-love-carlo-acutis-heres-why.

[23] Ibid.

[24] Ibid.

[25] The National Eucharistic Revival project began in 2022 on the feast of Corpus Christi and ends with the National Eucharistic Congress in 2024. The official website for the Eucharistic Revival is https://www.eucharisticrevival.org.

[26] Gregory Smith, "Just One-Third of U.S. Catholics Agree with Their Church That Eucharist Is Body, Blood of Christ", Pew Re-

search Center, August 5, 2019, https://www.pewresearch.org/fact-tank/2019/08/05/transubstantiation-eucharist-u-s-catholics/.

[27] Courtney Mares, "Relics of Carlo Acutis Brought to Poland in Hope of Inspiring Young Catholics", Catholic News Agency, May 17, 2021, https://catholicnewsagency.com/news/246908/relics-of-carlo-acutis-brought-to-poland-in-hope-of-inspiring-young-catholics.

[28] Stefano Lorenzetto, "Antonia Salzano: 'Il miracolo di Carlo Acutis, mio figlio, morto 15enne di leucemia: Un santo per il web'", *Corriere della Sera*, September 4, 2020, https://tinyurl.com/2p9bwn9p.